A Treatise on Lust and Illusion

A TREATISE ON LUST AND ILLUSION

Lewis Worrow

Contents

Foreword

The delusion of love, and its intertwined nature with lust, is a force that demands attention. It serves as a product of both physiological and psychological investment, essential in fulfilling the biological imperative. The following discourse represents the culmination of my own journey and offers a fresh perspective on the topic.

Throughout this exploration, we shall examine the use of social labels, the concept of morality within relationships, the institution of marriage, the reasons for its failure, and the significance of promiscuity and casual sex in men's lives. Moreover, we shall explore the consequences of poaching and the necessary circumstances in which relationships should be terminated.

I anticipate that these ideas will elicit hostility and accusations, as is to be expected. However, I assure you, dear reader, that the content of this work is grounded in empirical evidence. My goal is not to convince you, but to encourage you to reflect, reconsider, and contemplate the very nature of love. Whether you agree or disagree, the success of this book will depend on its ability to facilitate this process.

Origins of Mating Behaviour

1. Human mating behaviour is a complex and often a perplexing phenomenon that is widely discussed and regulated across all cultures. It can result in both joy and distress, but its intricacies are not easily comprehended.

1.1 Despite our desire for lasting and fulfilling relationships, conflicts and disillusionment are common occurrences, leading to high rates of divorce and infidelity. These struggles challenge our idealised views of love and commitment.

1.2 The prevailing belief that discord and dissolution in relationships are abnormal and personal failures is mistaken. Rather, conflict is a pervasive and typical aspect of mating behaviour that defies simple explanations.

1.3 Love, with its essential elements of commitment, tenderness, and passion, is a universal and enduring feature of human experience that is central to poetry, music, and literature across cultures.

1.4 Our lack of understanding of the paradoxical nature of human mating is costly both scientifically and socially. We require insight into the profound love we seek and the conflicts that challenge our cherished relationships, which may require exploring our evolutionary past to grasp the deep-seated grooves and strategies that have shaped our minds and bodies.

2. Charles Darwin's theory of sexual selection offers an explanation for the development of characteristics in animals that would appear to hinder their survival, by positing that these characteristics evolved because

they led to reproductive success in competition for a desirable mate.

2.1 Sexual selection takes two forms: intrasexual competition, in which members of the same sex compete with each other for greater sexual access to members of the opposite sex, and intersexual competition, in which members of one sex choose a mate based on their preferences for particular qualities in that mate.

2.2 The theory of sexual selection was resisted by mainstream social scientists for over a century due to its portrayal of human nature as instinctive and its implication that females have too much power in the mating process.

2.3 The field of evolutionary psychology emerged in the late 1970s and 1980s to identify underlying psychological mechanisms that are the products of evolution, and to explain the extraordinary flexibility of human behaviour and the active mating strategies pursued by women and men.

2.4 The largest study ever undertaken on human mating desires involved 10,047 persons worldwide, spanning thirty-seven cultures located on six continents and five islands.

2.5 The findings from this study and subsequent studies contradicted conventional thinking about men's and women's sexual psychology and forced a radical shift in perspective.

2.6 In the ruthless pursuit of sexual goals, men and women derogate their rivals, deceive members of the opposite sex, and even subvert their own mates, highlighting the competitive, conflictual, and manipulative aspects of human mating.

3.   Human mating and romance are strategic activities, not random or indiscriminate.

3.1 Sexual strategies are evolved solutions to the problems of successful mating.

3.2 Adaptations are human solutions to the problems of existence posed by nature.

3.3 Sexual strategies are tailored to specific adaptive problems and are driven by psychological mechanisms.

3.4 Information and cues from the external world inform our psychological mechanisms.

3.5 Sexual strategies do not require conscious planning or awareness.

4.   Desire for potential mates varies and is not equal across the board.

4.1 Sexual desires are similar to other desires, which have evolved to solve survival problems.

4.2 Food preferences illustrate how evolutionary processes shaped our desires.

4.3 The same evolutionary processes apply to our desires for a mate.

4.4 Selecting a mate who can provide resources and protection is critical for survival and reproduction.

4.5 Mate preferences have evolved to bestow reproductive advantages.

4.6 Women, like other animals, have evolved preferences for certain desirable qualities in a mate.

4.7 People's desires for commitment in long-term mating vary.

4.8 Short-term flings and temporary liaisons require different preferences than long-term relationships.

4.9 Universal preferences exist for certain characteristics in a mate, and these preferences reflect evolutionary logic.

5. Desirable characteristics increase demand for individuals.

5.1 Successful mating requires more than appreciation of traits.

5.2 Mating involves competition for desirable mates.

5.3 Elephant seal males compete for access to females.

5.4 Male success in competition is linked to passing on genes.

5.5 Female elephant seals choose winners to mate with.

5.6 Female preference determines competition among males.

5.7 Human mating behaviour differs from elephant seals.

5.8 Males must compete to attract females.

5.9 Competition among females is also intense in many species.

5.10 Women compete for access to males in human mating systems.

5.11 Tactics for competition are often determined by opposite-sex preferences.

5.12 Failure to possess desired traits may lead to exclusion in mating.

6. Retaining a mate is a crucial adaptive problem.

6.1 For the Plecia nearctica, or lovebug, successful reproduction depends on the male's ability to retain his mate and prevent rivals from fertilising her eggs.

6.2 Humans also face the challenge of holding onto a long-term mate, with infidelity risking the loss of resources, commitment, and investment in offspring.

6.3 Jealousy evolved as a psychological strategy to combat infidelity, motivating actions such as vigilance or violence.

6.4 Jealousy is not a fixed instinct, but rather sensitive to context and environment, with a range of behavioural options available to serve the strategy.

6.5 The various manifestations of jealousy are documented in this book, illustrating the flexibility and complexity of this psychological strategy.

7. Not all mates are worth retaining, and sometimes it is necessary to end a relationship due to lack of support, abuse, or sexual infidelity.

7.1 Remaining in a bad relationship does not aid in the successful passing on of genes.

7.2 In the animal kingdom, some species, such as ring doves, will break up due to infertility, serving the goal of reproduction better.

7.3 Humans have evolved strategies for selecting and retaining good mates, as well as jettisoning bad ones through divorce, which is a human universal found in all cultures.

7.4 The decision to leave a relationship is complex and involves weighing the costs and benefits inflicted by the mate, as well as the potential damage caused to oneself, children, and extended kin.

7.5 Breaking up is not simple, and requires negotiation and justification.

7.6 Humans often re-enter the mating market after a breakup, but this poses its own unique set of problems, such as age, assets, and liabilities.

7.7 Women often suffer more when it comes to remarrying after a divorce, especially if they have children from a previous relationship.

8. The pursuit of sexual strategies often creates conflict between members of different sexes.

8.1 In the scorpion fly, male courtship involves presenting a nuptial gift, which the female consumes while copulating with the male.

8.2 Male scorpion flies have evolved to select a nuptial gift that takes approximately twenty minutes for the female to consume, in order to ensure successful copulation.

8.3 Conflict arises when the gift is either too small or too large, leading to incomplete copulation or a fight over leftovers.

8.4 In human mating, men and women often have differing proclivities for brief or lasting sexual relationships, leading to conflicts in sexual strategies.

8.5 Immediate sexual gratification interferes with prolonged courtship, leading to conflict between men and women's goals.

8.6 Conflicts between men and women can persist throughout marriage, involving issues of emotional constrictions, sexual withholding, and infidelities.

8.7 Knowledge of our evolved sexual strategies can lead to minimising conflict and promoting harmony between the sexes.

8.8 Understanding sexual strategies is a step towards reducing conflict and fostering solutions for better relationships between men and women.

9. Our modern conditions of mating differ from ancestral conditions, but the same sexual strategies

operate with unbridled force due to our evolved psychology of mating, which remains unchanged.

9.1 Fast food chains serve food preferences that evolved in a past environment of scarcity, but we overconsume these elements due to their evolutionarily unprecedented abundance, which now hurts our health.

9.2 Our taste preferences and fear of snakes provide a window for viewing what ancestral conditions must have been like, and we carry equipment designed for an ancient world.

9.3 Our evolved mating strategies, just like our survival strategies, may currently be maladaptive in the currencies of survival and reproduction, such as the advent of AIDS rendering casual sex far more dangerous.

9.4 Humans have a large repertoire of mating strategies that are highly sensitive to context, including individual and cultural circumstances critical for evoking particular sexual strategies from the entire human repertoire.

9.5 The ratio of sexes and available men relative to available women is an important contextual factor that shifts men's and women's sexual strategies in a complex reciprocal relation based on the sex ratio.

9.6 To understand human sexual strategies, we must identify the recurrent selection pressures or adaptive problems of the past, the psychological mechanisms or strategic solutions they created, and the current contexts that activate some solutions rather than others.

10. Our cognitive and perceptual mechanisms are designed to perceive events within a limited time-span, which impedes our understanding of long-term evolutionary processes.

10.1 The historical misuse of biological explanations for political ends does not justify rejecting evolutionary theory.

10.2 The naturalistic fallacy confuses scientific description with moral prescription, and the antinaturalistic fallacy creates idealistic visions of human behaviour.

10.3 Behaviour is a joint product of evolved psychological mechanisms and environmental influences.

10.4 Environmental intervention can alter behaviour patterns, and natural selection did not create invariant instincts in humans.

10.5 Evolutionary psychology does not imply inequality between the sexes, restrict gender roles, or support stereotypes and exclusion of women from power and resources.

10.6 Evolutionary psychology strives to illuminate evolved mating behaviour, without prescribing what the sexes could or should be or offering political agendas.

10.7 Conflict, competition, and manipulation also pervade human mating, in addition to love and satisfaction.

What Women Want

11. Women's preferences in a mate have puzzled male scientists and other men for centuries.

11.1 Women's desires are more complex and enigmatic than the mate preferences of either sex of any other species.

11.2 Discovering the evolutionary roots of women's desires requires going far back in time, before humans evolved as a species, before primates emerged from their mammalian ancestors, back to the origins of sexual reproduction itself.

11.3 One reason women exert choice about mates stems from the most basic fact of reproductive biology-the definition of sex.

11.4 Men produce millions of sperm, while women produce a fixed and unreplenishable lifetime supply of approximately four hundred ova.

11.5 Fertilisation and gestation, key components of human parental investment, occur internally within women.

11.6 Women bear the exclusive burden of lactation, an investment that may last as long as three or four years.

11.7 Among some species, males invest more in parental care.

11.8 However, among all four thousand species of mammals, including the more than two hundred species of primates, females bear the burden of internal fertilisation, gestation, and lactation.

11.9 Women's great initial parental investment makes them a valuable but limited resource.

11.10   Ancestral women risked enormous investment as a consequence of having sex, so evolution favoured women who were highly selective about their mates.

11.11   Ancestral women who were indiscriminate experienced lower reproductive success, and fewer of their children survived to reproductive age.

11.12   Modern birth control technology has altered these costs, allowing women to have short-term dalliances with less fear of pregnancy.

11.13   Human sexual psychology evolved over millions of years to cope with ancestral adaptive problems.

11.14   Our underlying sexual psychology persists even though our environment has changed.

12.   In the selection of a mate, women tend to prefer men who display attributes that provide benefits, and tend to avoid those who impose costs.

12.1   These attributes may include physical prowess, athletic skill, ambition, industriousness, kindness, empathy, emotional stability, intelligence, social skills, sense of humour, kin network, and position in the status hierarchy.

12.2   However, preferences for certain attributes do not necessarily solve the problem of choosing a mate, as each woman must evaluate her unique circumstances and personal needs.

12.3   Furthermore, women must be able to identify and correctly evaluate cues that signal whether a man possesses a particular resource.

12.4   Integration of knowledge about a prospective mate is also necessary, as certain attributes are granted more weight than others in the final decision.

12.5   The heavily weighted component in the decision-making process tends to be the man's resources.

12.6 The evolution of a preference for generosity in a mate is driven by its repeated benefits over time, and its observable and reliable cues.

12.7 However, preferences for other attributes beyond generosity are individualised, personalised, and contextualised, and may not be adaptively relevant.

12.8 Gauging a man's mating value requires assessing not only his current position, but also his future potential.

12.9 The problem of choosing a mate calls upon psychological mechanisms that evaluate the relevant attributes and give each its appropriate weight in the whole.

13. Traditional societies suggest that ancestral men had clearly defined status hierarchies with resources flowing to those at the top.

13.1 Women desire men with high social status because it is a universal cue to the control of resources.

13.2 Social status provides access to better food, territory, health care, and social opportunities for children, as well as more and higher quality mates.

13.3 American women rate social status as important or indispensable, whereas men rate it as merely desirable.

13.4 Women place great value on education and professional degrees in mates, which are strongly linked with social status.

13.5 Women shun men who are easily dominated or fail to command the respect of the group.

13.6 Women seek "eligible" men, meaning those without committed resources, and value social status in a prospective mate across cultures.

13.7 Women solve the adaptive problem of acquiring resources by preferring men with high status as a cue to the ability to invest in them and their children.

14. Age is an important cue to a man's access to resources, as seen in both baboons and human societies.

14.1 In the Tiwi tribe, older men wield power and control the mating system.

14.2 Women prefer men who are older than they are in all cultures, with an average age difference of roughly three and a half years.

14.3 Women may value older mates due to their access to resources and their maturity and stability.

14.4 Younger women may prefer men a few years older who have promising futures.

14.5 Exceptions to the preference for older men occur when men possess powerful cues to status and resources, when older women lack bargaining power, or when women have high status and resources of their own.

14.6 The possession of economic resources, social status, and older age all contribute to a man's ability to acquire and control resources that women can use for themselves and their children.

14.7 In cultures where people marry young, the target of selection cannot be financial resources per se, but instead, a man's promise and key personality characteristics that indicate their ability to acquire future resources.

14.8 Women who value the personality characteristics likely to lead to status and sustained resource acquisition are better off than those who ignore these cues.

15. A study was conducted by Liisa Kyl-Heku and myself to identify tactics used by individuals to elevate their position in hierarchies in the workplace and social settings.

15.1 Eighty-four individuals from California and Michigan were asked to write down observed acts of people they knew well in getting ahead.

15.2 Using statistical procedures, twenty-six distinct tactics were discovered, including deception, social networking, sexual favours, education, and industriousness.

15.3 212 individuals in their middle to late twenties were asked which tactics they use to get ahead, and their spouses were asked which tactics their partners use to get ahead.

15.4 Correlation of this information with past and anticipated income and promotions showed that sheer hard work was one of the best predictors of success.

15.5 Industrious and ambitious men secure a higher occupational status than lazy, unmotivated men.

15.6 Women desire men who display ambition and industriousness and view it as important or indispensable, as supported by cross-cultural and cross-time evidence.

15.7 Women's preference for ambition and industriousness in men evolved as a means to obtain reliable resources, and it helped gauge the likelihood of obtaining future resources from a man. Dependability and stability are also cues to potential resources.

16. In a global study on mate selection, dependable character and emotional stability or maturity were rated highly after love.

16.1 Women, in all cultures, value these qualities in a potential partner, with dependability being valued more highly than men in most cultures.

16.2 Women's preference for these characteristics may stem from their reliability in providing resources consistently over time, while undependable partners inflict heavy costs.

16.3 Emotionally unstable men, as defined by themselves, their spouses, and interviewers, are especially costly to women, exhibiting possessiveness, dependency, verbal and physical abuse, and moodiness.

16.4 These costs indicate that such spouses fail to channel resources consistently over time, and their unpredictability can impede solutions to critical adaptive problems.

16.5 Emotional stability and dependability are broad categories that involve specific behaviours, with emotionally stable behaviour involving resiliency and a steady work ethic, while emotionally unstable behaviour reflects inefficiency in working, difficulty in handling stress, and a proclivity to inflict costs on others.

16.6 Women value dependability and emotional stability to avoid these costs and ensure a partner's ability to acquire and maintain resources for use by them and their children.

16.7 In human ancestral times, women who chose stable, dependable men had a greater likelihood of avoiding costs inflicted by undependable and unstable men.

17. Intelligence is an important cue of the acquisition and steadiness of resources.

17.1 People who score high on intelligence tests tend to have better education and higher paying jobs.

17.2 Intelligence predicts career advancement and higher income even in professions like construction and carpentry.

17.3 In tribal societies, the head men are usually among the more intelligent members of the group.

17.4 Women could have evolved a preference for intelligence in a potential mate as it predicts economic resources.

17.5 Women rank education and intelligence fifth out of eighteen desirable characteristics, and second out of thirteen.

17.6 Women value intelligence more than men in ten out of thirty-seven cultures.

17.7 Intelligent partners offer benefits such as good parenting skills and capacity for cultural knowledge.

17.8 Women who select intelligent mates are more likely to receive all critical resources.

17.9 Intelligent people tend to have a wide perspective, good social skills, efficient problem solving, and good money management.

17.10 Less intelligent partners may incur costs such as lack of social adeptness and poor problem-solving skills.

17.11 Ancestral women who preferred intelligent mates raised their odds of securing resources for themselves and their children.

17.12 Intelligence is moderately heritable, providing added benefits.

17.13 Similarity in intelligence is critical for successful mating.

18. Successful long-term mating requires a sustained cooperative alliance with another person for mutually beneficial goals.

18.1 Relationships riddled with conflict impede the attainment of those goals.

18.2 Compatibility between mates involves a complex mesh between two different kinds of characteristics.

18.3 Complementary traits involve a mate's possession of resources and skills that differ from one's own, in a kind of division of labour between the sexes.

18.4 Compatibility also requires traits that are most likely to mesh cooperatively with one's own particular personal characteristics and thus are most similar to one's own.

18.5 Discrepancies between the values, interests, and personalities of the members of a couple produce strife and conflict.

18.6 Couples who are mismatched in these regards tend to break up more readily than their matched counterparts.

18.7 The solution to the problem of compatibility is to search for the similar in a mate.

18.8 People seek mates with similar political and social values, race, ethnicity, religion, intelligence, and personality characteristics.

18.9 The similarity in compatible couples is in part a by-product of the fact that people tend to marry others who are in close proximity and those who are nearby tend to be similar to oneself.

18.10 Women express a preference for mates who are similar to themselves in many respects, including personality traits and intelligence.

18.11 The search for a similar other provides an elegant solution to the adaptive problem of creating compatibility within the couple.

18.12 Matched couples maximise the smooth coordination of their efforts when pursuing mutual goals such as child rearing, maintaining kin alliances, and social networking.

18.13 Seeking similarity prevents couples from incurring costs such as wasted energy, confusion, and incompatible goals.

18.14 The search for similarity solves several adaptive problems simultaneously, including maximising the value one can command on the mating market and reducing the risk of later abandonment or dissolution of the relationship.

18.15 Resources, personality, intelligence, and similarity provide important information about the benefits a potential partner can bestow.

18.16 Physical characteristics of a potential mate also provide adaptively significant information that has joined the array of preferences that women hold.

19. Women tend to prefer mates who display physical and athletic prowess, as seen in the case of Magic Johnson, which is a prevalent preference throughout the animal world.

19.1 Female frogs use a bump test to assess a male's physical ability to perform the function of protection.

19.2 Physical and sexual domination of females by males is a recurrent part of our primate heritage.

19.3 Female baboons exchange sex for protection from males.

19.4 Women prefer mates who offer physical protection, which is evidenced by their preference for tall, physically strong, and athletic partners.

19.5 Tall men tend to have a higher status in nearly all cultures and are more sought after in women's personal advertisements.

19.6 Men's physical attributes, such as size, strength, and athletic prowess, as well as good health, signal high mating value to women.

19.7 The preference for physical attributes that signal high mating value may have evolved as a response to the presence of aggressive men who tried to dominate women physically and sexually.

20. Across thirty-seven different cultures, women consistently prioritise good health in their choice of mate.

20.1 Poor physical conditions are seen as unattractive, from bad grooming habits to venereal diseases.

20.2 Behaviour can also signal good health, such as a lively mood and high energy level.

20.3 The importance of good health is not unique to humans, as animals display costly yet attractive traits signalling vitality.

20.4 The peacock's flamboyant plumage signals good health by carrying fewer parasites.

20.5 Ancestrally, choosing an unhealthy mate put women and their families at risk of disease, diminished the mate's ability to provide essential functions and benefits, increased the risk of premature death, and risked passing on genes for poor health to offspring.

20.6 A preference for healthy mates solves the problem of mate survival and ensures a steady flow of resources.

21. Men's possession of assets does not guarantee their commitment to a woman and her children, as some prefer to avoid marriage and seek temporary partners.

21.1 Women have a reasonable expectation of commitment from men due to the costs they bear through sex, pregnancy, and childbirth.

21.2 Acts of commitment, such as giving up other romantic relations and discussing marriage and children, are central to love and signal the intention to commit resources to one woman and her children.

21.3 Love is universal and experienced by people in all cultures worldwide, and is an important cue to commitment.

21.4 Women place a premium on love to secure the commitment of men's economic, emotional, and sexual resources, and require love even if all other desirable qualities are present.

21.5 Sincerity and kindness are critical to securing long-term commitment, with women seeking these qualities more frequently than men.

21.6 Kindness signals a willingness to commit energy and resources selflessly to a partner, while the lack of kindness signals selfishness and an inability or unwillingness to commit.

21.7 Requiring love, sincerity, and kindness helps women solve the adaptive problem of securing the commitment of resources from a man that can aid in the survival and reproduction of her offspring.

22. Women's preference for men with resources has been explained through the structural powerlessness theory, which suggests that women seek out powerful, high-status men due to their exclusion from power and resources.

22.1 The society of Bakweri in West Africa challenges this theory by demonstrating that when women have real power and access to resources, they still prefer mates with resources.

22.2 Even financially successful women in the US place a high value on a potential mate's earning capacity and social status.

22.3 Men's drive to control resources and exclude other men from power can be explained by evolutionary psychology, as men who failed to accumulate resources historically failed to attract mates.

22.4 Women's preferences for mates have shaped men's physical and social characteristics over millions of years.

23. Women choose their mates judiciously because they possess valuable reproductive resources.

23.1 Ancestral women faced great costs in failing to exercise choice, such as beatings, food deprivation, and abandonment.

23.2 Selecting a long-term mate involves at least a dozen distinct preferences, each corresponding to a resource that helps women solve critical adaptive problems.

23.3 Women's mating preferences are keyed to qualities that signal the likely possession or future acquisition

23.4 of resources, such as ambition, status, intelligence, and age.

23.5 Women seek love and sincerity as solutions to the commitment problem, as sincerity signals the man's capability of commitment and acts of love signal that he has committed to a particular woman.

23.6 Women selected men with strength and prowess as they offered protection and ensured the security of resources and commitment.

23.7 A man's health and similarity of interests and traits with his mate are important factors for women to ensure the convergence of mutually pursued goals.

23.8 Women's current mating preferences correspond with the multiple facets of adaptive problems that were faced by our women ancestors thousands of years ago.

23.9 Ancestral men had a different set of adaptive problems and viewed potential mates through a different lens.

Men Want Something Else

24. The puzzle of why men marry can be solved by considering the ground rules set by women.

24.1 Ancestral women required reliable signs of male commitment before consenting to sex, which made it costly for most men to pursue a short-term mating strategy exclusively.

24.2 The costs of not pursuing a permanent mate may have been prohibitively high for most men in the economics of reproductive effort, and failure to seek marriage could impair the survival and reproductive success of the man's children.

24.3 The absence of a father's investment could hurt children without fathers, as both teaching and political alliances help to solve mating problems later in life.

24.4 Evolutionary pressures operating over thousands of generations gave an advantage to men who married, due to the benefits of prolonged investment from two parents or related kin.

24.5 The economics of the mating marketplace typically produce an asymmetry between the sexes in their ability to obtain a desirable mate in a committed versus a temporary relationship.

24.6 Ancestral men sought a long-term mate with the capacity to bear children, and mechanisms evolved to sense cues to a woman's underlying reproductive value.

24.7 Youth and health are two observable cues to a woman's underlying reproductive value that ancestral men preferred.

25. Men's preference for younger women is a universal phenomenon and is based on the critical cue of women's reproductive value declining with age.

25.1 The preferred age difference between men and women in the United States is around 2.5 years, and men universally express a desire for mates who are younger than they are.

25.2 Men's preoccupation with a woman's youth is not limited to Western cultures but is also prevalent in other tribal peoples such as the Yanomamo Indians of the Amazon.

25.3 Men from thirty-seven cultures express a desire for wives approximately 2.5 years younger than themselves, with some cultural variations in the strength of this preference.

25.4 Men's preference for younger women is reflected in their actual marriage decisions worldwide, with grooms exceeding their brides in age by an average of three years.

25.5 This preference for younger women is based on a psychological preference inherited from male ancestors that focuses on a woman's reproductive value.

26. Men's preferences for youthful women are linked to reproductive capacity.

26.1 Evolutionary logic leads to universal standards of beauty that embody cues to female reproductive capacity.

26.2 Observable evidence of a woman's health and youth constitutes the ingredients of male standards of female beauty.

26.3 Ancestral men evolved a preference for women who displayed physical and behavioural cues of youth and health.

26.4 Universal cues to youth and health, such as clear skin and good muscle tone, are attractive, while cues to ill health or older age are seen as less attractive.

26.5 Standards of beauty emerge early in life, as evidenced by infants' social responses to faces.

26.6 Consensus exists across races and cultures about who is and is not attractive.

26.7 Symmetrical faces are considered more attractive because they provide a cue to the individual's health status and degree of perturbation during development.

26.8 Standards of attractiveness embody cues to health and youth, which emerge early in life, and are universal across races and cultures.

27. Facial beauty is not the only factor in determining a woman's reproductive capacity. Cultural standards of bodily attractiveness vary and are linked to social status.

27.1 Men do not have an innate preference for a specific body fat percentage, but rather for the features associated with social status in their culture.

27.2 Studies show that American women believe men prefer thinner women than is actually the case.

27.3 Men's preference for body size may vary, but their preference for a particular waist-to-hip ratio remains constant across cultures.

27.4 The waist-to-hip ratio is an accurate indicator of reproductive and long-term health status in women, making it a reliable cue for ancestral men's preferences in a mate.

27.5 Men find women with a low waist-to-hip ratio to be the most attractive, regardless of their total amount of body fat.

27.6 The waist-to-hip ratio is also important because it signals health and lack of current pregnancy in women.

28. Men prioritise physical appearance in mate preferences due to evolutionary cues and societal standards.

28.1 American men consistently rate physical attractiveness and good looks as more important in a potential mate than women.

28.2 The importance of attractiveness has increased in the United States due to media depictions of attractive models.

28.3 Despite changes in mate preferences over time, the sex difference in the importance of physical attractiveness remains constant and consistent across cultures.

28.4 Men's preference for physically attractive mates is a universal psychological mechanism that transcends culture.

29. The importance men place on a woman's attractiveness serves a critical role in social status, reputation, and hierarchies.

29.1 Elevated rank has been an important means of acquiring resources that make men more attractive to women.

29.2 A man's concern with his mate's effect on his social status is reasonable, given the consequences for gaining resources and mating opportunities.

29.3 Tangible characteristics such as ornamentation signal a person's status and resource holdings, which cannot be directly observed.

29.4 Men seek attractive women not only for their reproductive value but also as signals of status to same-sex competitors and other potential mates.

29.5 The case of Jim illustrates the value of an attractive wife as a social asset, which can delay divorce despite incompatibility and different values.

29.6 Trophy wives increase the status of the man who can win them.

29.7 Experiments show that men with attractive spouses are rated most favourably on criteria related to status, such as occupational prestige.

29.8 People suspect that a homely man must have high status if he can interest a stunning woman.

29.9 Dating someone who is physically attractive greatly increases a man's status, whereas it increases a woman's status only somewhat.

29.10 Men across cultures value attractive women not only for their reproductive capacity but also because it signals status.

30. Homosexual relationships can shed light on the evolutionary basis of sex differences in mate preferences.

30.1 The percentage of homosexuals in a given culture is difficult to determine due to issues with definitions.

30.2 Men who prefer women as mates may engage in homosexual behaviour for various reasons.

30.3 The origins of homosexuality are currently unknown, and theories such as kin selection have not been supported by evidence.

30.4 Studies have shown that homosexual men place a premium on youth and physical appearance in their mate preferences, similar to heterosexual men.

30.5 Lesbians, on the other hand, place little emphasis on physical appearance and prioritise other characteristics such as personality traits.

30.6 Youth is a key ingredient in the definition of beauty for male homosexuals, and physical attractiveness is the key determinant of desirability in the gay mating market.

30.7 Male homosexuals and male heterosexuals have similar mating preferences, except for the sex of their preferred partner.

31. Men generally value youth and beauty in a mate, but not all men are successful in attaining their desired partners.

31.1 Men with low status and resources may have difficulty attracting young and attractive women, while high-status men historically secured younger brides.

31.2 Kings and high-status men in various societies have maintained harems of young and pretty women and had sex with them frequently.

31.3 In modern America, high-status men such as rock stars and movie stars often choose partners who are two to three decades younger.

31.4 Men with higher occupational status are more likely to marry physically attractive women.

31.5 Men with higher income tend to seek younger partners, while men with lower income tend to seek partners closer to their own age.

31.6 Actual mating decisions are influenced by various factors, including preferences, age, and appearance.

31.7 Men with the means to do so often marry young, attractive women, which has historically led to greater reproductive success.

32. Advertisers use images of beautiful, young women to sell products because it exploits men's evolved psychological mechanisms and sells easily.

32.1 Images of highly attractive women can lead to decreased commitment, satisfaction, and closeness to current romantic partners in men.

32.2 Unrealistic images of beauty in media can create sources of unhappiness and interfere with existing real-life relationships.

32.3 Men's evolved standards of beauty and women's competitive mating mechanisms are exploited on an unprecedented and unhealthy scale in media images, leading to potential damage inflicted on both men and women.

32.4 Selecting a reproductively valuable woman does not guarantee exclusive paternity, leading to the critical adaptive problem of ensuring paternity.

33. Female mammals exhibit vivid visual cues and strong scents during estrus, whereas women possess concealed ovulation.

33.1 The lack of visible cues during ovulation creates a unique paternity problem for men.

33.2 Marriage provides a solution by increasing a man's certainty of paternity through repeated sexual contact.

33.3 Men seek qualities in a potential mate that increase the odds of securing their paternity, including premarital chastity and post-marital sexual loyalty.

33.4 Men value chastity in a potential mate more than women do, but the value has declined with cultural changes and availability of birth control.

33.5 Cultural variability in the value placed on chastity is influenced by factors such as economic independence of women and competition for husbands.

33.6 Future fidelity is a more important cue to the certainty of paternity than virginity per se, and promiscuity is seen as especially undesirable in a permanent mate.

33.7 Men place a high value on sexual loyalty and fidelity in a committed mateship.

33.8 A woman's future sexual conduct remains a significant factor in men's marriage decisions.

34. The emphasis on physical appearance in men's preference for a mate is not a universal law of the animal world, as demonstrated by other species such as peacocks and primates.

34.1 Human males have evolved a unique sexual psychology, placing a premium on physical appearance and youth to gauge a woman's future reproductive potential.

34.2 These evolved preferences for physical attractiveness and youth are universal across cultures, even in homosexual mate preferences.

34.3 The pursuit of physical attractiveness and youth in mating is not exclusive to Western culture or social conditioning, but rather ingrained psychological mechanisms.

34.4 Women's declining reproductive value with age is a product of evolution, and the cosmetics industry

34.5 profits from women's efforts to fight against this decline.

34.6 Suppressing the truth about evolved mate preferences is unlikely to change them, just as suppressing preferences for ripe fruit is unlikely to change taste preferences.

34.7 Standards of attractiveness reflect cues to youth and health, and hence reproductive value, rather than being arbitrary.

34.8 Cultural and economic conditions play a critical role in the importance placed on chastity, highlighting the sensitivity of mate preferences to context.

34.9 Sexual fidelity tops the list of men's long-term mate preferences, even in the face of birth control technology.

34.10 The existence of mate preferences for fidelity suggests that both sexes engaged in short-term mating and casual sex in ancestral times, pointing to the importance of exploring this aspect of human sexuality.

Casual Sex

35. When asked for casual sex, men are more likely to say yes than women.

35.1 Ancestral women likely engaged in casual sex at least some of the time, as opportunities for it would have disappeared otherwise.

35.2 In ancestral environments, hunting opened up opportunities for extramarital sex due to a lapse in scrutiny from a woman's regular mate.

35.3 Despite the prevalence and evolutionary significance of casual sex, most research on human mating has focused on marriage.

35.4 Our lack of knowledge about casual mating is partly due to deeply held values that shun promiscuity and infidelity.

35.5 The taboo surrounding casual sex fascinates us, and we should investigate why it plays such a significant role in our mating repertoire.

36. Our psychology, anatomy, physiology, and behaviour are shaped by prior selection pressures.

36.1 Physiological clues reveal an ancient history of short-term sexual strategies.

36.2 Men's testes size is a clue to multiple matings and intense sperm competition.

36.3 Men's relatively large testes suggest women in human evolutionary history sometimes had sex with more than one man.

36.4 Human testicular volume is smaller than that of the highly promiscuous chimpanzee, suggesting our human ancestors rarely reached the chimpanzee's extreme of promiscuity.

36.5 Sperm production and insemination also provide clues to the existence of casual mating and marital infidelity.

36.6 Men's sperm count increases when separated from their partners, suggesting a history of casual sex.

36.7 Women's orgasm functions to increase the probability of conception, and the number of sperm retained is linked to whether they are having an affair.

36.8 Women time their adulterous liaisons to coincide with ovulation, suggesting evolved reproductive strategies for their own benefit.

36.9 These physiological mechanisms suggest a long evolutionary history of casual mating.

37. Anatomical and physiological features are not the only clues to human casual mating history.

37.1 There are psychological mechanisms that suggest a past of casual sex.

37.2 Men and women have evolved different mechanisms due to different adaptive benefits of temporary liaisons.

37.3 For men, the primary benefit of casual sex is an increase in offspring, which results in a need for sexual access to a variety of women.

37.4 Men have evolved psychological mechanisms that cause them to seek multiple sexual partners, including old-fashioned lust.

37.5 Men desire more sexual partners than women, as evidenced by a study of American college students.

37.6 Men's inclination to count their "conquests" and to "put notches on their belt" is an adaptation to brief sexual encounters.

37.7 Men let little time elapse before seeking sexual intercourse to mate with a larger number of women.

37.8 Men are more likely to consent to sex with someone they desire, even after a short period of acquaintance, than women.

38. Men's desire for casual sex partners can lead them to relax their standards for acceptable partners, including age, intelligence, personality, and marital status.

38.1 College men generally accept a wider age range for temporary liaisons than women do, with men willing to mate with individuals as young as sixteen and as old as twenty-eight.

38.2 Men are willing to overlook a variety of desirable characteristics in a casual mate, including charm, athleticism, education, generosity, honesty, independence, kindness, intellectuality, loyalty, sense of humour, sociability, wealth, responsibility, spontaneity, cooperativeness, and emotional stability.

38.3 Men generally have fewer objections to undesirable characteristics in casual partners than women do, such as mental abuse, violence, bisexuality, dislike by others, excessive drinking, ignorance, lack of education, possessiveness, promiscuity, selfishness, lack of humour, and lack of sensuality.

38.4 Men view sexual experience and promiscuity as desirable traits in a temporary sex partner, but as undesirable in a long-term commitment.

38.5 Men seeking casual sex partners are less concerned with commitment and are less likely to view a woman's marital status as a barrier to casual sex.

38.6 These findings suggest that men's relaxation of standards for casual sex partners reflects a strategic approach to gain sexual access to a variety of partners, potentially influenced by evolutionary history.

39. The Coolidge effect is a psychological solution to the problem of gaining sexual access to multiple women.

39.1 This effect refers to the tendency of males to be sexually rearoused upon the presentation of novel females, giving them a further impulse to gain sexual access to multiple women.

39.2 The Coolidge effect is a widespread mammalian trait that has been documented many times.

39.3 Sexual arousal to novelty occurs despite attempts to diminish it.

39.4 Men across cultures also show the Coolidge effect.

39.5 The frequency of intercourse with one's partner declines steadily as the relationship lengthens in Western culture.

39.6 The waning of lust for one's wife promotes a roving eye.

39.7 Human roving takes many forms.

39.8 More men have extramarital affairs more often and with more partners than women.

39.9 Spouse swapping in America is nearly always initiated by husbands.

39.10 Group sex is sought out mainly by men.

39.11 Sexual desires vary from person to person and from culture to culture.

39.12 Women's sexual attractiveness varies from "flavourless" to "delicious".

39.13   The charm of novelty in sexual desire gradually slips away, leaving behind the eternal monotony of passion.

39.14   The human male would be promiscuous in his choice of sexual partners throughout the whole of his life if there were no social restrictions.

39.15   The human female is much less interested in a variety of partners.

40. Sexual fantasies can offer insight into men's preference for casual mating, as seen in videos that depict men with multiple women.

40.1 Men have twice as many sexual fantasies as women and are more likely to dream about sexual events.

40.2 Men's sexual fantasies often involve strangers, multiple partners, or anonymous partners, with a focus on numbers and novelty.

40.3 Men's sexual fantasies prioritise physical aspects stripped of emotional context, with an emphasis on visual images.

40.4 Women's sexual fantasies often feature familiar partners and emphasise emotions and personal involvement.

40.5 Women pay more attention to their partner's responses than to visual images.

40.6 The language and assumptions used to describe sexual fantasies can limit or distort our understanding of love, desire, and illusion.

41. Men tend to view women as increasingly attractive as closing time at a bar approaches, regardless of alcohol consumption.

41.1 This shift in perception may be a result of a psychological mechanism sensitive to decreasing opportunities for casual sex over the course of the evening.

41.2 The "beer goggles" phenomenon may be more accurately attributable to this mechanism than to increased intoxication.

41.3 After orgasm with a casual sex partner, some men report a negative shift in attraction toward the partner.

41.4 This shift may be more common when a man is motivated primarily by desire for casual sex rather than a committed relationship, and when the woman with whom he has sex is lower in desirability on the mating market.

41.5 The negative shift in attraction may function to prompt a hasty departure in order to reduce the man's risk of unwanted commitment or reputational damage.

41.6 The speculation that male desire elevates a man's judgments of beauty prior to orgasm and then lowers his judgments of beauty following orgasm may have evolved as a mechanism for reaping the benefits of casual sex without paying the costs.

41.7 Further research is necessary to determine whether these shifts in emotions and perceptions are common and under which conditions they occur.

41.8 Our language and assumptions about love and desire may be limiting or distorting our understanding of these concepts.

42. Male homosexuality provides insight into the nature of sexual desire unclouded by the compromises imposed by the opposite sex's sexual strategies.

42.1 Male homosexuals frequently engage in casual sex with strangers and search for new and varied sex partners, while lesbians are more likely to settle into intimate, lasting, committed relationships with fewer partners.

42.2 Homosexual proclivities reveal fundamental differences between men and women in the centrality of casual sex.

42.3 Prostitution is a reflection of men's greater desire for casual sex, with men overwhelmingly the consumers.

42.4 The prevalence of prostitution is a consequence of men's desire for low-cost casual sex and women's either choosing or being forced by economic necessity to offer sexual services for material gain.

42.5 Father-daughter incest is far more common than mother-son incest, with men heavily concentrated among stepfathers as perpetrators.

42.6 Men's quest for sexual variety and attractive casual partners is revealed in the patterns of incest.

42.7 Sexual fantasy, the Coolidge effect, lust, the inclination to seek intercourse rapidly, shifts in judgments of attractiveness, homosexual proclivities, prostitution, and incestuous tendencies all betray men's strategies for casual sex.

42.8 Men's strategies for casual sex are rooted in an evolutionary past that favoured those with short-term mating in their sexual repertoire.

42.9 Heterosexual men require the consent of women for casual sex.

43. Women's benefits from short-term mating have been overlooked, as their reproductive success is not dependent on multiple partners.

43.1 However, women can gain immediate access to resources through casual sex, as evidenced by traditional societies and prostitution.

43.2 Women's preferences for short-term partners reveal their desire for economic resources and the ability to evaluate potential long-term partners through sexual compatibility and personality assessment.

43.3 Women view pre-existing committed relationships and promiscuity in potential partners as highly undesirable, as they signal unavailability as a long-term mate and interfere with the ability to extract immediate resources.

43.4 Women's desires for a short-term sexual partner and a husband are remarkably similar, including qualities such as kindness, romance, stability, health, humour, and generosity.

43.5 Men's preferences, however, drastically differ in the context of mating.

43.6 The consistency of women's preferences in both contexts suggests that women see casual partners as potential husbands and thus maintain high standards for both.

43.7 Casual sex allows women to more accurately assess their own mating value and avoid underestimating their worth.

43.8 Women also benefit from having a second mate for protection, particularly in societies where they are vulnerable to violence or rape.

43.9 Women may use casual sex to secure back-up protection against conflicts and have men waiting in reserve.

43.10 Evidence shows that casual sex can serve a mate-switching function, allowing women to replace a mate quickly without incurring the costs of starting over.

43.11 Casual sex can elevate women's status and potentially help them secure a more desirable husband.

43.12 Women may also use casual sex to gain superior genes for their children, particularly through the "sexy son hypothesis."

43.13 The preference for physically attractive casual partners may be a psychological clue to a human evolutionary history in which women benefited through the success of their sexy sons.

43.14 Arranged marriages restrict women's opportunities for short-term mating, but women can still benefit through personal choices such as clandestine affairs or elopements.

44. All sexual strategies carry costs, including casual sex which can lead to sexually transmitted diseases, a bad reputation, or even physical harm.

44.1 Infidelity can lead to violent retaliation from jealous partners and even murder.

44.2 Women bear greater risks of reputational damage and physical harm in short-term sexual encounters.

44.3 Women who adopt a short-term sexual strategy are at greater risk of physical and sexual abuse due to the lack of a permanent mate to offer protection.

44.4 Mate preferences can help minimise the risks of abuse and violence.

44.5 Unmarried women who engage in casual sex risk pregnancy without the benefits of an investing partner.

44.6 Infanticide is sometimes committed by single women in the absence of an investing man.

44.7 Unfaithful married women risk losing resources from their husbands and wasting valuable reproductive time.

44.8 Short-term mating presents hazards for both sexes, but psychological mechanisms have evolved to minimise costs and maximise benefits.

45. Sexual behaviour varies among individuals, and is influenced by social, cultural, and ecological factors.

45.1 The absence of an investing father during childhood increases the likelihood of casual sex in women, as does experiencing divorce during childhood.

45.2 Casual sex is also related to one's developmental stage in life, with adolescents using temporary mating as a means of experimentation and clarification of preferences.

45.3 Transitions between committed matings also offer opportunities for casual sex, allowing individuals to reassess their value on the mating market.

45.4 The abundance or dearth of eligible men relative to eligible women is another critical context for temporary mating.

45.5 In cultures where food is shared communally, women have less incentive to marry and often shift to temporary sex partners.

45.6 Future desirability as a mate also influences the likelihood of casual sex, with men at the apprenticeship stage of a promising career and women with low current desirability being more likely to pursue short-term relationships.

45.7 Legal, social, and cultural sanctions may also encourage short-term mating.

45.8 The sexual strategies pursued by others also affect the likelihood of casual sex.

45.9 Casual sex is influenced by various contexts and factors, and should be understood within the broader repertoire of human sexual strategies.

46. disregarding human anatomy, physiology, and psychology that indicate a history of affairs.

46.1 The advantages of affairs for men may have blinded scientists to the potential benefits for women, who participate willingly and demand benefits.

46.2 This understanding of human nature may be unsettling, with men hopping into bed with near strangers and wives scanning the mating terrain and sometimes cuckold husbands.

46.3 However, this complex repertoire of potential mating strategies provides greater power, flexibility, and control over our destiny.

46.4 People can choose from a large mating menu and tailor their strategies to the contexts they encounter, thanks to modern technology and contemporary living conditions.

46.5 Effective birth control allows for avoiding unwanted pregnancies, while geographic mobility and government safety nets lower the restrictive influences on mating decisions.

46.6 Recognising the complexity of our mating strategies may conflict with socialised ideas of matrimonial bliss, yet it provides greater power to design our own mating destiny than ever before.

Attracting a Partner

47. Knowing one's desired qualities in a mate does not guarantee success in obtaining that mate. Success is dependent on signalling that one can provide the benefits desired by a potential mate.

47.1 Men and women have evolved motivations to acquire and display the characteristics most sought after by the opposite sex. These motivations result in competition to attract a mate by besting one's rivals in desirable qualities.

47.2 Derogatory tactics can be effective in attracting a mate because they exploit psychological mechanisms that predispose individuals to be sensitive to certain valuable qualities in potential partners.

47.3 The success of attraction and derogatory tactics depends on whether the target is seeking a casual or committed relationship. Men and women tailor their techniques accordingly.

47.4 The rules of play differ in the sexual field compared to the marriage market. Casual affairs increase opportunities for deception, especially in domains important to the opposite sex.

47.5 More men than women seek casual sex partners, creating a hurdle for men as there are fewer willing women. Women tend to have more control in short affairs.

47.6 Attracting a mate requires display of desirable qualities, which differ between men and women due to their differing desires.

48. The display of resources for attracting mates is pervasive in the animal kingdom, as evidenced by the male roadrunner's offering of a kill to a female.

48.1 Men employ various tactics for displaying their resources to attract mates, including bragging about accomplishments, displaying wealth, and derogating rival's resources.

48.2 Women are less likely to derogate a rival's resources, and timing plays a key role in the effectiveness of different resource display tactics.

48.3 Wearing expensive clothing is an effective tactic for attracting both casual and permanent partners.

48.4 The importance of resources in attraction is not limited to Western cultures, as seen in the Siriono of eastern Bolivia.

48.5 The power of imparting resources for attraction is a longstanding phenomenon, as seen in the observations of Ovid two thousand years ago.

49. Displays of commitment, such as love, devotion, and persistence, are powerful attractions for women as they signal a willingness to channel time, energy, and effort over the long run.

49.1 The reliability of these signals renders them especially effective in attracting women, as they are difficult and costly to fake.

49.2 Men who show commitment are more likely to be interested in long-term relationships and are thus more effective at courting women as permanent mates.

49.3 Acts of kindness, nurturance towards children, and displays of loyalty and fidelity are all effective tactics for signalling commitment and attracting women.

49.4 Men who feign long-term intentions or deceive women about their true intentions use simulation of commitment as a tactic to gain access to short-term sex.

49.5 Honesty is a powerful tactic for obtaining a permanent mate, as it conveys that the man is not simply seeking a transient sex partner.

49.6 Prior commitments and signals that resources are already committed elsewhere undermine attraction, as they indicate a man's unwillingness to channel resources exclusively to the woman.

49.7 Signals of commitment help men to attract women because they match what women want in a long-term sexual partner.

50. Men use displays of physical and athletic prowess as a tactic to attract women.

50.1 Women use these tactics less frequently and less effectively.

50.2 These tactics are more effective for attracting casual sex partners than spouses.

50.3 Derogation tactics, including putting down rivals' strength and athletic ability, are more effective in short-term mating contexts.

50.4 In traditional societies, a man's physical feats determine his status and reproductive success.

50.5 Displays of physical and athletic prowess remain powerful attractions in both traditional and modern societies.

50.6 The effectiveness of these tactics for men depends on the context of women's desires.

50.7 Our language and assumptions about love and desire may limit or distort our understanding of these concepts, including the ways in which physical prowess is used to attract mates.

51. Masculine self-confidence is effective for attracting mates, particularly in casual mating contexts.

51.1 Self-confidence signals status and resources, which can lead to success in finding temporary sex partners.

51.2 Women distinguish genuine self-confidence from false bravado and are more attracted to the former.

51.3 Men with high self-esteem tend to approach physically attractive women for dates, regardless of their own physical attractiveness.

51.4 Rejection can produce a downward cycle of resentment and hostility, leading to lowered confidence and a change in sexual tactics.

51.5 Feigning confidence is a tactic used by men to appear more masculine and assertive around women, increasing their odds of securing casual sex.

51.6 Displays of bravado and confidence are also directed towards other men in an attempt to elevate status and prestige within the group.

51.7 This tactic is subject to exploitation by other males, as seen in the satellite or sneak strategy used by bullfrogs and sunfish.

51.8 College men sometimes use this tactic to poach mates, including feigning femaleness or homosexuality.

51.9 Our language and assumptions about love and desire may limit our understanding of these concepts, as they are shaped by social and evolutionary factors.

52. Men's successful attraction tactics depend on women's desires, while women's tactics depend on men's preferences.

52.1 Women who embody physical and behavioural cues that signal youth and attractiveness are seen as reproductively valuable and have a competitive edge.

52.2 Women heavily compete to enhance their physical appearance along youthful and healthful lines, supported by the cosmetics industry.

52.3 Women use cosmetics and beauty products to trigger men's attraction, applying rouge, skin creams, hair products, and even undergoing surgery to meet men's evolved desires.

52.4 Women spend significantly more time and effort enhancing their appearance than men, and improving appearance is more effective for women in attracting sex partners than marital partners.

52.5 Women also use derogation tactics to manipulate their appearance and denigrate other women's looks, which is more effective for women in temporary and sexual contexts than in long-term and marital contexts.

52.6 Modern cosmetology exploits women's desire to appear attractive through visual media and technology, creating a runaway beauty competition that exploits women's autonomy and choice in deploying attraction tactics.

52.7 Advertisements exploit women's evolved concern over appearance and raise the standards of attractiveness to which women aspire, distorting women's and men's understanding of the actual mating pool and mating market.

52.8 Every living human is an evolutionary success story, the product of a long and unbroken line of successes in the five-million-year Pleistocene beauty contest of sexual selection.

53. Women seeking a long-term partner prioritise displays of fidelity, as it signals a commitment to the relationship without deception or pursuing other men.

53.1 Studies confirm the effectiveness of fidelity, devotion, and avoiding sex with other men as the top tactics for attracting a permanent mate.

53.2 Fidelity also solves a crucial reproductive problem for men: ensuring paternity.

53.3 Women derogate rivals by questioning their loyalty and promiscuity, which can be effective for attracting a long-term partner but risky for a man seeking casual sex.

53.4 The prevalence of derogatory terms for female promiscuity in language reinforces its abhorrence by committed men and its use by women to undermine rivals.

53.5 The tactic of acting coy or unavailable is more effective for women in the context of permanent mates, signalling both desirability and fidelity.

53.6 Women with a history of promiscuity may have difficulty appearing faithful and loyal, as reputation plays a crucial role in mate selection.

54. In casual mating relationships, men primarily desire sex with attractive women, making sexual overtures and signalling sexual availability powerful tactics for women.

54.1 These attraction tactics are judged to be more effective for women in casual than in permanent contexts, and they are substantially more effective for women than for men in the short term.

54.2 Sexualising appearance and initiating visual contact also prove to be highly effective tactics for women seeking short-term relations.

54.3 However, initiating visual contact may be less effective for a woman seeking a long-term rather than short-term mate because it signals low desirability and perhaps gives a cue to future infidelity.

54.4 Women also use derogatory tactics to question the sexual accessibility of rivals, implying an exploitative strategy of feigning sexual accessibility but then failing to deliver.

54.5 Women may act submissive, helpless, and even stupid to attract short-term mates, conveying to the man that he need not expect hostile reactions to his advances and implicitly giving men permission to approach.

54.6 Signals of sexual accessibility may be part of a larger strategy to lure a man into a long-term relationship, as once a woman gains sexual access to a man of her choice, her proximity offers opportunities for gradually escalating both the benefits he will receive by staying in the relationship and the costs he will incur if he leaves her.

55. Success in mating relies not only on understanding a potential partner's context and intentions, but also on outdoing the competition.

55.1 Men and women enhance their own attractiveness and derogate their rivals to attract a mate.

55.2 In casual sex, men deceive women by feigning commitment and faking characteristics sought by the opposite sex to achieve a quick gain.

55.3 Women retaliate by insisting on stronger cues to commitment and feigning interest in casual sex to conceal their long-term intentions.

55.4 Women offering sexual bait may risk their chances of finding a long-term partner, as men abhor promiscuity and indiscriminate sexual activity in a mate.

55.5 Both men and women are aware of the possibility of deception from the opposite sex and use tactics to prevent it.

55.6 The sex ratio affects the tactics used to attract a mate.

55.7 In areas where the sex ratio is imbalanced, competition is fiercer and the pool of eligible mates is smaller for women due to their high standards.

55.8 Those who succeed in attracting a mate must then deal with the challenge of maintaining a lasting relationship.

Staying Together

56. The benefits of committed partnerships are numerous, including complementarity of skills, a division of labour, resource sharing, a unified front against enemies, a stable home environment for children, and extended kin networks.

56.1 Retaining a committed partner is crucial to reaping these benefits, as failure to stay together results in significant costs such as loss of extended kin bonds, essential resources, and a stable home environment for children.

56.2 Men risk losing valuable childbearing capabilities and maternal investment if they fail to prevent the defection of their mate, while women risk losing access to their mate's resources, protection, and paternal investment.

56.3 Both men and women incur costs from failing to keep a mate because of lost opportunities for exploring other mating possibilities.

56.4 Mate-keeping tactics are important in animal mating systems, with insects providing useful contrasts to humans due to the diversity of their tactics.

56.5 Insects use tactics such as concealing the mate from competitors and physically preventing a takeover by other males.

56.6 Although humans differ from insects in their use of psychological manipulation to retain a mate, both sexes are equally invested in mate-keeping efforts due to the reproductive rewards of staying together.

56.7 Continuing to fulfil a partner's desires and deploying mate-guarding strategies are important human strategies for mate keeping, with sexual jealousy serving as a mechanism to regulate these strategies.

57. The problem of uncertain paternity is a common issue for males whenever fertilisation and gestation occur inside the female's body, which is exacerbated when males invest in offspring after they are born.

57.1 Men invest heavily in their offspring compared to many other male mammals, making cuckoldry a serious adaptive problem that men throughout human evolutionary history have had to solve.

57.2 Effective psychological mechanisms for solving the paternity problem and for reducing the likelihood of cuckoldry have evolved in our ancestors, with sexual jealousy providing direct evidence of this mechanism.

57.3 Sexual jealousy consists of emotions that are evoked by a perceived threat to a sexual relationship, leading to actions designed to reduce or eliminate that threat.

57.4 Cuckolded men risk not only suffering direct reproductive costs but also losing status and reputation, which can seriously impair their ability to attract other mates.

57.5 Both men and women experience jealousy with equal frequency and intensity, serving as a key psychological mechanism that becomes activated in response to a threat to a valued relationship.

57.6 Men's jealousy is triggered primarily by cues to the possible diversions of their mate's sexual favours to another man, while women's jealousy is triggered by cues to the possible diversion of their mate's investment to another woman.

57.7 Physiological distress patterns in men and women illustrate the precision with which humans have adapted over time to the particular threats they have faced to keeping a mate.

57.8 Sexual differences in the causes of jealousy appear to characterise the entire human species.

58. Male sexual jealousy is a common cause of violence towards wives, including murder.

58.1 Homicides by women also often stem from male sexual jealousy.

58.2 Sexual jealousy is a leading motive behind homicide in many cultures.

58.3 The adaptive function of jealousy to prevent infidelity and ensure paternity may explain extreme jealousy.

58.4 Killing a spouse may have been reproductively beneficial in some circumstances in our evolutionary past.

58.5 Jealousy often leads to efforts to fulfil the desires of one's mate to maintain the relationship.

59. When one's mate is threatened, jealousy can motivate tactics directed at the mate, rival, or oneself.

59.1 Men and women use a variety of tactics to keep a mate, which are based on their mate's initial desires and preferences.

59.2 Fulfilling a mate's initial preferences and desires is highly effective in preserving the relationship, according to mate-keeping studies.

59.3 Men who provide love, kindness, and helpfulness to their mates succeed in retaining their mates, as judged by an effectiveness rating of 6.23 on a 7-point scale.

59.4 Men who fail to perform acts of love and commitment have wives who contemplate or seek divorce more than those whose husbands are kind and loving.

59.5 Men who provide economic and material resources to their mates also succeed in retaining them, with an average effectiveness rating of 4.50.

59.6 Women enhance their physical appearance to keep their mates, which is the second most effective tactic after love and kindness, and exploits men's desire for physical attractiveness.

59.7 Successful tactics for keeping a mate fulfil the desires of the opposite sex, which includes women's preference for economic and material resources and men's preference for physical attractiveness.

59.8 Language and assumptions about love, desire, and illusion can shape our understanding of these concepts, and may be limiting or distorting our perception of them.

60. In desperate attempts to keep their partners, people may resort to emotional manipulation tactics such as crying, guilt-tripping, and dependency.

60.1 Submission and self-abasement are also common tactics, with men using them 25% more than women to retain their partners, regardless of relationship length.

60.2 The reason for this sex difference is unknown and requires further research.

60.3 Provoking sexual jealousy is another tactic, with women being twice as effective as men in retaining their partners.

60.4 Women may intentionally elicit jealousy to test their partner's commitment and elevate their levels of possessiveness.

60.5 This tactic is more likely to be used by women who perceive themselves as more involved in the relationship and more desirable than their partners.

61. Humans and other species display possessive attitudes towards their possessions and mates.

61.1 Public marking is a common method of signalling ownership and deterring intrasexual competitors.

61.2 Public signals of possession can be verbal, physical, or ornamental.

61.3 Our panel of raters judged these public signals to be more effective for men in keeping their mates than for women.

61.4 Public signals provide a strong cue to women of a man's intent to commit, fulfilling women's long-term desires.

61.5 Maintaining vigilance, detecting signs of defection, and conveying a message of commitment to a mate were common tactics used by both sexes to keep their mates.

61.6 Concealing mates and monopolising a mate's time were also tactics used to decrease contact with rivals and prevent poaching on mates.

61.7 Historical and cross-cultural precedents show that mate monopolisation and mate concealing have been practised through claustration, veiling, and harems.

61.8 Public signals and tactics for keeping mates serve the goal of preventing contact between mates and potential rivals.

61.9 Men historically had more power, which allowed them to use drastic tactics to limit women's freedom of choice.

61.10　In modern industrial societies, both sexes use public signals to retain their mates, typically less drastic than those used by medieval lords.

62. To keep mates, individuals may inflict costs on competitors or mates through derogation, threats, and violence, which contrast with benefit-conferring tactics.

62.1 Destructive tactics deter rivals from poaching on mates and mates from straying, rendering rivals less attractive and increasing the likelihood of couples remaining together.

62.2 Verbal denigration, belittling appearance or intelligence of a competitor, and damaging rumours are mild forms of derogation, whereas threats and violence are more costly.

62.3 These tactics are performed mostly by men and convey a message to other men that they will incur a heavy cost if they show interest in a mate.

62.4 Punishing a mate who shows interest acquires effectiveness from the deterrent value of threatened costs, which can be physical or psychological, and may involve terminating the relationship itself.

62.5 Genital mutilation and infibulation in various cultures effectively prevent extramarital sexual activity.

62.6 Men may inflict extreme costs on women, including violence and jealousy-driven attacks, to keep them.

62.7 Sexual jealousy exists in every culture, and wives are regarded as chattel to be owned and controlled, with cuckoldry representing the unlawful stealing of another man's resources.

62.8 Legal strictures reflect an intuitive understanding of human evolutionary psychology and the importance of protecting resources.

63. The ability for two individuals without shared genes to remain in a lasting union is a remarkable feat, but the fragility of this bond presents unique challenges.

63.1 Successful solutions to these challenges involve the provision of necessary resources to prevent defection, keeping competitors at bay, emotional manipulation, and, unfortunately, destructive measures.

63.2 These tactics are effective because they exploit psychological mechanisms in both mates and rivals.

63.3 Beneficial tactics, such as giving love and resources, work by fulfilling psychological desires, while enhancing physical appearance works because of the psychological desire for attractiveness.

63.4 However, tactics of threats and violence work by exploiting fear and can lead to conflict.

63.5 Male sexual jealousy, a major mechanism for staying together, is also responsible for a majority of violence against mates.

63.6 This mechanism causes destruction because of high reproductive stakes and conflicting interests.

63.7 Tactics of staying together can lead to conflict between the sexes.

Sexual Conflict

64. Novels, songs, and media often depict conflicts between men and women, focusing on the pain and suffering they inflict upon each other.

64.1 Individuals were asked to list all the actions of the opposite sex that upset or angered them, resulting in 147 distinct items ranging from insults to sexual infidelity.

64.2 Studies of dating and married couples reveal that conflict between the sexes stems from evolved mating strategies and occurs when one person interferes with another's goal.

64.3 Conflict arises when men compete for the same resources, such as access to a desirable woman, or when one sex interferes with the other's goals and preferences in the sexual arena.

64.4 Conflict serves no evolutionary purpose and is often an undesirable outcome of different sexual strategies.

64.5 Negative emotions, such as anger and distress, have evolved as psychological solutions to alert individuals to interference with their sexual and adaptive goals and lead to action to eliminate the problem.

64.6 Men and women differ in which events activate negative emotions based on their sexual strategies. Men seeking casual sex without commitment often anger and upset women, while women withholding sex after leading men to invest will cause men to get angry and upset.

65. Conflict between men and women often arises due to disagreements about sexual access.

65.1 Men tend to be more selective about whom they invest in, and seek sexual access with a minimum of investment.

65.2 Women, on the other hand, often seek to obtain investment or signals of investment before giving a man sexual access.

65.3 Differences in perception of one's value as a mate can lead to conflict between individuals.

65.4 Men tend to infer sexual interest on the part of a woman more often than women do.

65.5 Women sometimes use their sexuality as a means of manipulation.

65.6 Sexual pushiness can lead to sexual aggressiveness, which can have a significant negative impact on women.

65.7 Men tend to underestimate how upsetting sexual aggression is to women, which can lead to further conflict.

65.8 Sexual withholding can also lead to conflict between men and women, as men tend to pursue casual sex while women tend to be more selective.

65.9 Withholding sexual access can impose a cost on men and is experienced as upsetting, which can lead to further conflict.

66. Adaptive problems can be solved through one's own labour or by securing the labour of others.

66.1 Securing the labour of others, with a minimal commitment, is often more successful in solving life's adaptive problems.

66.2 It is often in a woman's best interest to have a man devoted to her and her children, while a man benefits from allocating resources to multiple adaptive problems.

66.3 Conflict over commitment arises between sexes, with women expressing irritation over men's emotional constrictedness.

66.4 Women desire men to express their emotions openly, but men may benefit from withholding expression to channel resources towards other adaptive problems.

66.5 Men's reproductive resources are more easily fractionated than women's, giving men a strategic advantage.

66.6 Concealing sexual strategies through emotional concealment allows men to maintain strategic advantage.

66.7 Women analyse and agonise over the available signs to discern where men stand, causing conflict over commitment.

66.8 Women use tactics, such as getting men to express themselves emotionally, to gain access to important information about a man's degree of commitment.

66.9 Men commonly complain that women are too moody and emotional, absorbing time and effort.

66.10 Women use moodiness as an assessment device to test the strength of the bond and elicit commitment from men.

66.11 Psychological mechanisms, such as conflict over emotional expression, remain hidden from view.

67. Couples conflict over the investment of time, energy, and resources.

67.1 Neglect and unreliability are manifestations of investment conflicts, with more women complaining about them than men.

67.2 Complaints about neglect and unreliability reflect a conflict over investment of time and effort.

67.3 Neglect signals a low investment, indicating a lack of commitment.

67.4 Complaints about investment conflicts do not end in marriage, with ongoing skirmishing and testing.

67.5 Women try to sequester their mate's investment, while men resist monopolisation and seek to channel effort towards other goals.

67.6 Selfishness and self-centeredness increase as courting signals subside and each partner becomes freer to indulge the self.

67.7 Married couples often fight over the allocation of money, with disagreements on spending and earnings.

67.8 Men complain more about their spouse's spending on clothes, while women complain more about their spouse's failure to channel money to them.

67.9 Conflict between the sexes corresponds to initial sex-linked preferences in a mate.

68. Deception is a prevalent phenomenon in both the plant and animal world, as well as in human mating.

68.1 Orchids, for example, deceive male wasps by mimicking the colours, shapes, and scents of female wasps, leading to cross-pollination.

68.2 In human mating, men and women sometimes deceive each other to gain access to resources that the other possesses.

68.3 Women are more likely to use sexual deception, such as flirting or using sexual cues to elicit resources, while men are more likely to use commitment deception, such as exaggerating their feelings to have sex.

68.4 Deception about the depth of commitment continues in the form of sexual infidelity among married couples, with women being more upset by emotional involvement in affairs.

68.5 The costs of being deceived about a potential mate's resources and commitment are shouldered more heavily by women.

68.6 Women have evolved strategies, such as imposing courtship costs and discussing details with friends, to guard against deception.

68.7 Men also cannot ignore deception at the hands of women, especially when seeking spouses.

68.8 Conflict between the sexes can take on violent forms, but understanding the sexually differentiated strategies underlying human mating can help mitigate such conflicts.

68.9 The language and assumptions we use about love, desire, and illusion may limit or distort our understanding of these concepts, as they are shaped by our cultural and evolutionary histories.

69. Abuse manifests in various forms, including psychological abuse that can result in partners feeling undervalued, less desirable, and with limited mating prospects if they were to leave the relationship.

69.1 Condescension and derogation are tactics utilised by abusers to achieve these goals, with women typically being the victims and men the perpetrators.

69.2 Newlywed men often perform acts of condescension towards their wives, thereby lowering their perception of desirability relative to that of their husbands.

69.3 Victims of abuse often increase their investment and commitment to the relationship to placate their abusers due to limited alternative mating options.

69.4 Men who physically batter women often do so to exert coercive control over them, with jealousy being a frequent cause of arguments that lead to abuse.

69.5 Spouse abuse is risky for abusers, as it may backfire and result in their partner's defection.

69.6 Wife abuse occurs across cultures, with the Yanomamo providing an example of husbands striking their wives as a sign of love.

69.7 Insults about physical appearance are another form of abuse used by men to lower women's perception of their own desirability.

69.8 Greater understanding of the contexts in which abuse occurs may lead to more effective means of reducing or eliminating it, with certain personality dispositions, discrepancies in desirability, and the absence of legal and other costs being potential factors affecting the incidence of wife battering.

70. Sexual access conflicts can occur in both romantic relationships and the workplace, leading to sexual harassment defined as unwanted sexual attention.

70.1 Sexual harassment creates conflict between the sexes, and evolutionary psychology may identify key psychological mechanisms and contexts that trigger this behaviour.

70.2 Sexual harassment is typically motivated by the desire for short-term sexual access and can disproportionately affect young, physically attractive, and single women.

70.3 Women's reactions to sexual harassment follow evolutionary psychological logic, with men having positive emotional reactions to casual sex, while women often feel insulted or uncomfortable being treated as mere sex objects.

70.4 Women's reactions to sexual harassment also depend on the status of the harasser, with advances from men of lower occupational status more upsetting.

70.5 Women's reactions to sexual harassment are also affected by the perceived motivation of the harasser, with short-term sexual and coercive intentions being more harassing than sincere romantic intentions.

70.6 However, not all women consider even coercive behaviour as harassment, as some may benefit from, or take advantage of, men's sexual advances.

70.7 These findings follow from the evolutionary logic of human mating strategies, but do not condone sexual harassment or overlook its harmful effects.

71. Rape is defined as the use of force or threat to obtain sexual intercourse.

71.1 Estimates of the number of women who have been raped vary depending on the researcher's definition.

71.2 Rape often occurs within the context of mating relationships, such as dating or marriage.

71.3 Men are almost always the perpetrators of rape and women the victims, pointing to a continuity with other conflicts between the sexes.

71.4 The evidence is controversial as to whether rape is an evolved strategy of men or a side effect of their general sexual strategy.

71.5 There is a correspondence between rape and men's evolved sexual psychology, as evidenced by the age distribution of rape victims and men's attraction to young and attractive women.

71.6 Men may use coercion and violence to achieve a variety of goals, including obtaining sexual access to young women.

71.7 Feminist investigations have illuminated the abhorrence of rape from the victim's point of view.

71.8 Psychological pain experienced by rape victims may be an evolved mechanism that focuses attention on the events surrounding the pain, promoting the elimination and avoidance of the pain-causing events.

71.9 Men who use coercion to get sex tend to exhibit distinct characteristics, including hostility toward women, endorsement of the myth that women secretly want to be raped, and a personality profile marked by impulsiveness, hostility, hypermasculinity, and high sexual promiscuity.

71.10 Culture and context heavily influence the occurrence of rape, such as in war contexts or among certain cultural practices.

72. Such conflicts arise due to the divergent mating strategies evolved by men and women.

72.1 These mating strategies lead to the development of psychological mechanisms, such as anger, sadness, and jealousy, that function to alert individuals to interference with their mating strategies.

72.2 Women's anger is evoked most intensely in situations where men interfere with their mating strategies, such as by acting condescending, abusive, or sexually aggressive.

72.3 Men's anger is most intensely evoked when women interfere with their mating strategies, such as by refusing sexual advances or engaging in infidelity.

72.4 These conflicts create a spiral of escalating and evolving strategies on both sides, with each sex developing increasingly sophisticated methods to achieve their mating goals and escape abuse from the other.

72.5 The adaptive emotions of anger and psychological pain help individuals reduce the costs of such interference.

72.6 In the context of dating or marriage, these emotions can lead to the termination of the relationship.

Breaking Up

73. Human mating is not necessarily a once-in-a-lifetime event, as divorce and remarriage are common, resulting in almost 50% of US children not living with both genetic parents and stepfamilies becoming more prevalent.

73.1 Divorce and the end of long-term mating relationships are universal across cultures, as seen in the high rates of divorce among the !Kung and Ache.

73.2 People end committed relationships for various reasons, such as when a spouse imposes costs or when a better mate opportunity arises.

73.3 Staying in a bad marriage can result in negative outcomes, such as lost resources, physical and psychological abuse, and inadequate child care.

73.4 Leaving a bad relationship can lead to benefits such as new mating opportunities, better resources, child care, and allies, which help in solving survival and reproduction problems.

74. In ancestral times, injury and death were recurrent hazards for mates, particularly for men engaged in physical combat and hunting.

74.1 Women, who were primarily gatherers, faced less danger but experienced high mortality rates during childbirth.

74.2 A mate's decline in value, potential death, or a rise in one's own desirability could lead to seeking alternative mates.

74.3 An increase in resources, status, or the presence of more desirable alternatives could also prompt leaving a long-term mate.

74.4 Humans likely evolved psychological mechanisms to assess the costs and benefits of relationships and identify potential alternatives.

75. Throughout human evolutionary history, dissolving a mateship presented a recurring adaptive problem, which imposed selection pressures for the evolution of strategic solutions.

75.1 People who failed to recognise a decrease in their mate's value, who did not prepare to remate in the event of a spouse's death, or who did not trade up to a higher quality mate would have been at a reproductive disadvantage.

75.2 People in committed relationships assess and evaluate other possible mates.

75.3 Discourse about potential mates allows for information exchange and assessment of the mating terrain.

75.4 Evaluating alternative mates occurs unconsciously, and decision-making may depend on these calculations.

75.5 Men and women compare potential mates with their current partner, and decisions to keep or leave a mate depend on these comparisons.

75.6 People typically require a clear justification for leaving a long-term mate, one that explains the breakup to others and minimises damage to social reputation.

75.7 Violating a partner's expectations for a mate would be an effective justification for expelling them.

75.8 Acts that violate universal preferences for kind and understanding mates are effective tactics for expelling a mate for both sexes.

75.9 Men and women evaluate changes in their mates over time by different standards, due to the sex differences in benefits from long-term matings in ancestral times.

75.10   Infidelity and infertility are the most common causes of divorce across cultures.

76. Adultery is the most pervasive cause of conjugal dissolution across eighty-eight societies.

76.1 In fifty-four societies, divorce occurs only if the wife is adulterous.

76.2 The double standard in reactions to unfaithfulness is observed globally, regardless of gender.

76.3 Women may tolerate infidelity more often because of the prohibitively high costs of divorce.

76.4 Men may have greater power to impose their will, which may force women to tolerate infidelity in their husbands.

76.5 A wife's unfaithfulness more often causes an irrevocable rift that ends in divorce.

76.6 People may use infidelity intentionally to get out of a bad marriage.

76.7 Infidelity is a justifiable cause of getting rid of a mate, and people may exploit it, even if no actual infidelity has occurred.

76.8 Pretending that an affair has occurred provides justification for breaking up, as infidelity is widely regarded as a compelling reason for ending a relationship.

77. The divorce rate for ring doves is around 25% per season, with infertility being the major cause of bond-breaking.

77.1 Human couples with no children are more likely to divorce than couples with two or more children.

77.2 Children create a genetic commonality that strengthens marital bonds and reduces the probability of divorce.

77.3 Infertility and adultery are the most frequently cited causes of divorce across cultures.

77.4 Sterility is a sex-linked issue, with women being blamed more than men in some societies.

77.5 Some cultures do not sanction divorce but may separate couples who do not produce children.

77.6 Old age is linked to lower fertility, with women being more affected than men.

77.7 The expectation is that older age in a wife leads to divorce more often than older age in a husband.

77.8 Infertility and infidelity are adaptive problems that exerted selection pressure on human ancestors for a psychology attuned to reproductive failures.

78. Sex is essential for reproduction and depriving a man of sex may result in a loss of reproductive dividends.

78.1 Sexual refusal by wives is a common cause of conjugal dissolution across twelve societies.

78.2 Women commonly employ tactics of sexual refusal to break up with unwanted mates.

78.3 One woman successfully ended her marriage by refusing her husband's sexual advances.

78.4 The assumption that women give sex to get love and men give love to get sex may limit our understanding of the complex dynamics of love and desire.

78.5 Our language and assumptions about love and desire may be distorting our understanding of these concepts.

79. A man's ability and willingness to provide resources is essential to his value as a mate for women, as well as his ability to attract and retain them.

79.1 Men who fail to provide these resources are often considered unfit for marriage and are more likely to experience divorce.

79.2 Inadequate economic support, housing, food, and clothing are all commonly cited as reasons for divorce, and these are solely attributed to men in every society.

79.3 Women who earn more than their husbands are more likely to seek divorce, as men who do not fulfil their role as a provider are viewed as less desirable.

79.4 Men who lack ambition or drink excessively may also be seen as unfit for marriage and maybe jettisoned by their partners.

80. Polygyny is a common practice in many cultures, with 83% of 853 analysed permitting it, and 25% of older men in some West African societies having multiple wives.

80.1 Even in cultures where it is not legally sanctioned, polygyny can occur, with 25,000 to 35,000 polygynous marriages estimated in the United States.

80.2 From a woman's perspective, the major drawback of polygyny is the competition for resources among wives and their children.

80.3 Co-wives may derive some benefits from each other's presence, but conflicts often arise, and polygyny has been found to cause divorce in twenty-five societies.

80.4 Conflict among co-wives may have been an adaptive problem in ancestral times, as polygynous men needed to keep all wives happy to maintain control.

80.5 Polygynous men adopt various tactics to minimise conflicts, such as strict resource distribution, equal attention, and equal sex, separate residences, and alternating days spent with each wife.

80.6 Sororal polygyny tends to minimise conflicts, which suggests genetic overlap creates a psychological convergence in the interests of women.

80.7 Despite efforts to keep peace, women in some societies leave their husbands when they indicate plans to acquire a second wife.

80.8 The difficulty of sharing a husband's time and resources with other women makes it challenging for wives to accept polygyny.

81. Kindness is highly valued in a committed mate worldwide because it signals a willingness to engage in a cooperative alliance, which is essential for long-term mating success.

81.1 Disagreeable people make poor mates because their irritable, violent, abusive, derogatory, neglectful, and alienating behaviour imposes severe costs psychologically, socially, and physically.

81.2 Cruelty, maltreatment, and ruthlessness rank among the most frequent causes of marital breakup in the cross-cultural study on conjugal dissolution, cited in fifty-four societies.

81.3 Adultery and sterility are the only sources of conjugal dissolution that exceed the frequency of cruelty, maltreatment, and ruthlessness in all cultures.

81.4 Unkindness and psychological cruelty may in some cases be related to events that occur during the course of a marriage, such as adultery and infertility.

81.5 Some forms of unkindness are evoked by reproductively damaging events that occur within the marriage.

81.6 In other cases, unkindness is a personality characteristic of one spouse that is stable over time.

81.7 The wives of disagreeable husbands tend to be dissatisfied with the marriage, and by the fourth year of marriage many seek separation and divorce.

81.8 One of the most effective tactics for getting rid of a bad mate is to act mean, cruel, caustic, and quarrelsome.

81.9 Cruelty and unkindness occur worldwide as a tactic for expelling a mate, which is the opposite of the kindness that is central to men's and women's preferences in a mate worldwide.

82. The major causes of marital dissolution throughout history have been events and changes that disrupt reproductive success and interfere with preferred mating strategies.

82.1 These events and changes include infidelity, infertility, sexual withdrawal, lack of economic support, acquisition of additional mates, and unkindness.

82.2 To maintain a lasting marriage, couples should remain faithful, produce children, have economic resources, be kind and understanding, and not refuse or neglect their partner sexually.

82.3 However, some damaging events or changes are beyond our control, such as infertility, disease, and death.

82.4 Psychological mechanisms for assessing potential mates cannot be turned off easily and often include comparisons with alternative prospects.

82.5 Hostile forces that threatened reproductive success in ancestral environments still exist today and activate psychological mechanisms for dealing with marital dissolution.

82.6 These mechanisms may cause people to seek new mates and sometimes divorce repeatedly as significant events emerge over a lifetime.

Changes Over Time

83. Yeroen, the dominant adult male among the chimpanzees at the Arnhem zoo colony, exhibited his dominance through physical displays and was responsible for 75% of matings.

83.1 Luit, a younger male, challenged Yeroen's status and eventually overthrew him, taking over as the dominant male and increasing his sexual access to females to over 50%.

83.2 Yeroen formed an alliance with Nikkie and together they were able to defeat Luit, allowing Yeroen to regain some sexual access with 25% of matings.

83.3 Humans, like chimpanzees, experience changes in mating value and have evolved psychological mechanisms to deal with these changes, motivating adaptive action.

83.4 Mating behaviour entails changes over time and clarifying one's mating desires takes time and practice.

83.5 The goal of this chapter is to describe the broader changes that occur in men and women's mating lives, including losses, triumphs, uncertainties, and inevitabilities.

84. A woman's desirability as a mate is primarily based on her reproductive value, which decreases with age.

84.1 This is exemplified in societies where women are purchased by men as brides, such as the Kipsigis in Kenya, where the bride price is based on the perceived quality of the bride's reproductive value.

84.2 Other factors that decrease a woman's value as a mate include poor physical condition, physical handicap, pregnancy, and prior children from another man.

84.3 The perception of attractiveness in women changes with age, with young women commanding the highest ratings and old women the lowest, due to universal psychological mechanisms that equate cues to youth with mate value.

84.4 Exceptions to this include women with status, fame, money, personality, or social networks who can remain desirable as they age, and a person's value as a mate is ultimately determined by their individual needs and circumstances.

84.5 From the wife's perspective, her reproductive success becomes increasingly linked with nurturing her children, while from the husband's perspective, her parenting skills are a valuable and virtually irreplaceable resource.

84.6 Older women can provide economic and domestic resources and become powerful political allies of their mates, but from the perspective of other men on the mating market, their value as a prospective mate is generally low due to decreased reproductive value and competing demands on their efforts. These changes can affect a marriage.

85. Over time, sexual dynamics within marriage shift, with men increasingly complaining about their wives withholding sex.

85.1 Complaints from both men and women about their partners refusing sex grow over time, but men voice this complaint more frequently.

85.2 Frequency of intercourse decreases with age, with women under nineteen having sex roughly 11-12 times a month, dropping to once a week after age 50.

85.3 The arrival of a baby can significantly reduce the frequency of sex.

85.4 Men's sexual interest and happiness in their sexual relationship with their spouse declines with age, especially if they perceive their wife's physical attractiveness has decreased.

86. Ageing men and women experience a decrease in sexual satisfaction and show distress with their partners' lack of affection and attention, indicating a decrease in commitment to the relationship.

86.1 Women are more distressed by declining affection than men, with complaints doubling after four years of marriage.

86.2 Women are also more disturbed by their partners' inattentiveness over time, while men show a parallel increase in distress.

86.3 Ignoring a spouse's feelings is another index of diminishing commitment, with women expressing more distress over time than men.

86.4 Men are more troubled by the growing demands for commitment from their wives, while women show equal vigilance in guarding their mates regardless of their age.

86.5 Men's efforts to guard their mates are most intense when their mates are youngest and most reproductively valuable.

86.6 The population of Trinidad exhibits this pattern of behaviour, with men spending more time with young and fecund mates.

86.7 In Middle Eastern societies, women are most heavily veiled and concealed when they are youngest, with men exhibiting homicidal rages over young wives.

86.8 The decrease in men's guarding zeal as women age is due to the decrease in women's reproductive capacity.

86.9 These examples demonstrate the ways in which our understanding of love and desire is shaped by societal and cultural norms and assumptions, which may limit or distort our understanding of these concepts.

87. Women's sexual behaviour with other men becomes less constrained as men's intense mate guarding lessens.

87.1 Reliable information on extramarital affairs is difficult to obtain, as secrecy surrounds the subject.

87.2 Extramarital affairs are underreported, and the actual incidence is likely higher than reported.

87.3 Women's incidence of extramarital sex shows a curvilinear relationship with age, peaking between ages thirty-one and forty.

87.4 Women's extramarital orgasms also show a curvilinear trend with age, peaking toward the end of their reproductive years.

87.5 Older women may be better able to take advantage of existing sexual opportunities and feel freer to pursue extramarital desires due to lower penalties for being caught.

87.6 Women may use affairs to switch mates before their reproductive value plummets.

87.7 Men engage in sex outside of marriage more often and consistently than women.

87.8 Men's greater desire for extramarital sex is reflected in studies showing a desire for it and a higher incidence of it.

87.9 Extramarital sex comprises a significant proportion of men's sexual outlets at every age throughout their life.

87.10 The increase in the importance of extramarital sex for men may result from boredom or a decrease in a wife's sexual attractiveness.

87.11 The proportion of men and women having affairs over their lifetimes depends on the nature of the mating system.

87.12 Men's sexual psychology disposes them to seek sexual variety, and men seek extramarital sex when the costs and risks are low.

87.13 Women also seek short-term sex, including extramarital sex, but their desires, fantasies, and motivations for this form of sex are less intense on average than men's.

88. Women experience a critical change in their sexual activities as they age, namely the cessation of direct reproduction, which occurs at menopause.

88.1 Menopause occurs much earlier in a woman's life than the end of life, unlike other primate species where the post-reproductive phase represents only 10% or less of their total lifespan.

88.2 Women's fertility declines sharply, in contrast to the gradual decline of other bodily functions with age, which requires explanation.

88.3 The theory that women's post-reproductive phase is a result of better nutrition and health care is unlikely, as the maximum human lifespan has not been altered by medical technology, and women's other vital capacities decline gradually as if designed for a longer lifetime.

88.4 Menopause is likely a female adaptation that prompts the shift from mating and direct reproduction to parenting, grandparenting, and other forms of investing in kin, as continuing to produce children would have interfered with an ancestral woman's reproductive success.

88.5 Older women tend to acquire wisdom and knowledge that are valuable to their children and grandchildren, increasing their control over resources and their ability to influence others, which can be channelled toward their genetic clan.

88.6 The grandmother hypothesis of menopause aligns with observations of increased investment in kin as women age, but requires more extensive testing.

88.7 Menopause may not be an adaptation, but an incidental by-product of early and rapid breeding, as producing many high-quality children early may wear out a woman's reproductive machinery.

88.8 Ancestral women were able to reproduce early and rapidly due to the tremendous parental resources provided by investing mates, which may have created propitious conditions for early and rapid reproduction.

88.9 The change in women's lives that produces a shift to investing in genetic relatives is directly linked to the high levels of parental investment by men, which in turn can be traced to women's active choosing of men who show the ability and willingness to invest, making reproductive changes intimately linked to mating relations.

89. Women's desirability as mates declines steeply with age, while the same does not apply to men's.

89.1 Men's value as mates is not closely or predictably linked with age due to qualities such as intelligence, cooperativeness, parenting proclivities, political alliances, kin networks, coalitions, and ability and willingness to provide resources to a woman and her children.

89.2 Men's resources and social status typically peak much later in life than women's reproductive value, and men differ more markedly from one another in the resources and social status they accrue.

89.3 Social status and possession of resources are separate qualities, and the distribution of social status by age can be observed in contemporary hunter-gatherer societies around the world.

89.4 Men and women of comparable age are not typically comparable in desirability due to the central ingredient of a woman's desirability being her reproductive value and a man's being his resource capacity.

89.5 Men diverge dramatically in their ability to accrue resources between the ages of twenty and forty, but there is tremendous variability in the individual circumstances of women who do the choosing.

89.6 Women's psychological mechanisms for selecting mates are highly sensitive to circumstances, and a man's willingness to parent can partially compensate for the lack of other qualities.

89.7 Our evolved psychological mechanisms tailor our choices over our lifetime to the individual circumstances in which we find ourselves.

90. Men have a higher mortality rate than women and die earlier in all societies.

90.1 Men are more susceptible to infections, suffer from a greater variety of diseases, and are involved in more accidents than women.

90.2 Men are also more likely to be murdered, commit suicide, and die while taking risks.

90.3 The higher mortality rate among men is directly related to their sexual psychology, which drives competition for mates.

90.4 In polygynous mating systems, males take greater risks to compete for and secure mates, leading to a shorter lifespan on average.

90.5 The reproductive stakes for men are higher than for women, resulting in more men risking being shut out of mating entirely.

90.6 Men who are at the bottom of the mating pool and therefore at risk of being shut out entirely are more likely to engage in risky behaviour, which can be lethal.

90.7 Men's evolved sexual psychologies are designed to respond to particular conditions by increasing the amount of risk they are willing to take.

90.8 The traits that yield success in competition among males for mates have been selected for at the expense of success at longevity.

90.9 In general, selection via intrasexual competition has been hard on men in terms of survival and longevity.

91. The mortality rate of men is a critical factor that creates an imbalance between the number of men and women in the mating market, referred to as the marriage squeeze.

91.1 This imbalance is affected by factors such as infant, childhood, adolescent, and adult mortality rates, emigration, and imprisonment, which result in a surplus of women on subsequent mating markets.

91.2 Divorce and remarriage patterns also contribute to the marriage squeeze, with men tending to remarry younger women than they are, and fewer women being able to obtain a second marriage partner than men.

91.3 The sexual psychology of men and women is at the heart of the marriage squeeze, with selection favouring ancestral men who preferred younger women as mates, and ancestral women who preferred older men with resources as mates.

91.4 Changes in the ratio of men to women throughout life affect the degree of selectivity and the sexual strategies of both sexes.

91.5 When there is a surplus of men, fewer men can be highly selective, and a low ratio of men restricts women's selectivity.

91.6 A dearth of available men causes women to take greater responsibility for providing resources and intensifies their competition with each other for male attention.

91.7 When men outnumber women, women can more easily exact what they want from men, and men become more competitive with each other to attract and retain desirable women.

91.8 However, an excess of men can also increase violence toward women and may promote sexual aggression and rape.

91.9 Our evolved mating strategies result in these changes over time in the mating market.

92. Human mating behaviour changes over a lifetime, influenced by reproductive value, status, and resources.

92.1 Women experience puberty earlier and have a shorter window for reproduction than men.

92.2 Women's reproductive value affects the behaviour of men in their social environment, leading to intense guarding in younger years and decreased attention in later years.

92.3 Men pursue extramarital affairs for sexual variety, while women do so for emotional goals and to switch mates.

92.4 Men who increase their status and resources remain desirable for mating, while those who fail to do so become side-lined.

92.5 Men's desire for younger women as they age reflects a universal desire with an evolutionary history.

92.6 Men die at an earlier age due to risk-taking behaviour and intrasexual competition for mating success.

92.7 Both sexes have evolved mechanisms to adjust mating strategies based on changes in sex ratios.

92.8 Despite the challenges, 50% of individuals remain together throughout their lifetimes, due to mechanisms promoting strategic harmony between the sexes.

92.9 As individuals age, they place less value on physical appearance in a mate and more value on enduring qualities important for successful marriages and investment in children.

Harmony Between the Sexes

93. Human sexual strategies are adaptable to social context, shaped by evolutionary mechanisms that offer a range of behavioural options for mating.

93.1 No behaviour in the sexual realm is inevitable or genetically predetermined.

93.2 Both men and women have agency in their sexual decisions, with the ability to tailor their mating choices to personal circumstances and desires.

93.3 Knowledge of the conditions that favour different mating strategies allows for conscious decision-making and the potential to change behaviour.

93.4 Understanding the adaptive functions of jealousy and other emotional responses can lead to creating relationships that minimise negative emotions and promote positive interactions.

93.5 Empirical studies provide a foundation for a theory of sexual behaviour that has broader implications for social interactions and relationships between men and women.

94. Understanding the relations between men and women requires recognition of both sexual similarities and differences.

94.1 Both sexes share many adaptive solutions to evolutionary problems, such as regulating body temperature and valuing intelligence and dependability in a mate.

94.2 However, sexual differences in psychology of mating arise from facing different adaptive problems over the course of evolution.

94.3 Men have evolved mate preferences for sexual loyalty, a psychology of jealousy centred on sexual infidelity, and a predisposition to withdraw commitment when cuckolded.

94.4 Women dislike being treated as sex objects or valued for qualities largely beyond their control, and men dislike being treated as success objects or valued for the size of their wallet and the importance of their status.

94.5 Assuming that men and women are psychologically the same goes against our evolved sexual psychology.

94.6 Men and women differ in their preferences for a mate, proclivities for casual sex without emotional involvement, desire for sexual variety, and tactics to attract, keep, and replace mates.

94.7 Denying or wishing away these differences will not make them disappear.

94.8 Harmony between men and women can only be approached when we confront and acknowledge the differing desires of each sex.

95. Feminist evolutionists have noted that the evolution of sexual differences has implications for feminism, as patriarchy, which involves the control of resources by men and the subordination of women, is considered a major cause of the battle between the sexes.

95.1 Human sexual strategies show that men tend to control resources worldwide and oppress women, sometimes through sexual coercion and violence, with a focus on women's sexuality and reproduction. Women also participate in perpetuating this oppression.

95.2 An evolutionary perspective on sexual strategies shows that men's dominant control of resources can be traced, in part, to women's preferences in choosing a mate, favouring men who possess status and resources.

95.3 Men form coalitions with other men for gaining resources, power, and sexual access to women, as seen in animals such as baboons, chimpanzees, and dolphins.

95.4 Women's preferences for a successful, ambitious, and resourceful mate and men's competitive mating strategies evolved together, leading to men's dominance in the domain of resources.

95.5 Women's continued preferences for men with resources and men's continued competition to acquire these resources are the same forces that contribute to maintaining resource inequality today.

95.6 Men's efforts to control female sexuality lie at the core of their efforts to control women, which can be explained by our evolved sexual strategies.

95.7 Men and women compete primarily against members of their own sex for resources and sexual access, with each individual sharing key interests with particular members of each sex and in conflict with others.

95.8 To achieve harmony and equality, women and men must be recognised as linked together in a spiralling co-evolutionary process that started with the evolution of desire and continues to operate today through our strategies of mating.

96. Sexual diversity is a crucial aspect of human mating strategies.

96.1 Differences in desires between men and women are not uniform but vary within each sex.

96.2 Contextual circumstances dictate individual preferences in mating strategies.

96.3 Societal value judgments about sexual behaviour may reflect selfish interests.

96.4 Casual sex is deeply rooted in human evolutionary history for both sexes.

96.5 Female choice in mating is a powerful evolutionary force often overlooked.

96.6 Women have specific psychological mechanisms designed for temporary mating.

97. The diversity of sexual strategies in humans is a reflection of our nature.

97.1 Acknowledgement and acceptance of sexual diversity can lead to greater harmony.

97.2 The diversity of human cultures is marked by differences in beliefs, values, and practices.

97.3 Such variations extend to human sexual behaviour, with different societies displaying different sexual strategies.

97.4 Evolutionary psychology posits that early experiences, parenting practices, and environmental factors shape an individual's sexual strategy.

97.5 Children raised in unstable homes are more likely to adopt a sexual strategy of early reproduction and rapid turnover, while those raised in stable homes adopt a strategy of committed, permanent mating.

97.6 The value placed on chastity varies across cultures, with some societies prioritising it as an indispensable quality in a mate, while others consider it unimportant.

97.7 Such differences can be attributed to early developmental experiences, with Chinese and Swedish societies offering contrasting examples.

97.8 The ratio of men to women is another critical factor that influences sexual strategy, with tribes such as the Ache and Hiwi displaying varying patterns of promiscuity and monogamy.

97.9 Cultural variations in mating behaviour are thus influenced by a combination of evolutionary psychology and cultural inputs.

97.10   All humans inherit a repertoire of possible sexual strategies from their ancestors.

98. Human mating involves competition and conflict, as desirable partners are outnumbered by those who desire them.

98.1 Women often compete to attract men who have superior resources, while men compete to attract women of striking beauty or with desirable characteristics.

98.2 Competition among individuals of the same sex is inevitable as long as people have mating desires and differ in the qualities desired by the opposite sex.

98.3 Conflict between the sexes arises from fundamental differences in mating strategies and desires.

98.4 Conflict within couples cannot be eliminated entirely, as unavoidable conditions may trigger it.

98.5 The fact that conflicts between men and women originate from our evolved mating psychology contradicts widely-held beliefs that such conflicts reflect a particular culture's practices.

98.6 Men's tendency to take physical risks in their pursuit of resources has led to the pernicious manifestation of warfare, which is almost exclusively a male activity.

98.7 The close connection between conflict within a sex and conflict between the sexes is revealed by the sexual motivation underlying violence.

98.8 Conflict between the sexes occurs between individual men and women interacting with each other socially.

98.9 There is no solidarity among all men or all women that creates conflict between the sexes.

98.10 By employing evolved mechanisms that are sensitive to personal costs, we may be able to reduce the expression of the more brutal aspects of our human repertoire.

99. Humans rely on one another for the continuation of their genes, and marital unions reflect a unique level of trust and reciprocity.

99.1 Sexual strategies play a defining role in human nature and are necessary for achieving lifelong love.

99.2 Children serve as a means to align the interests of a man and woman, fostering permanent bonds of marriage.

99.3 Sexual fidelity promotes trust and harmony between partners, while infidelity creates conflict and disrupts marital bonds.

99.4 Fulfilling each other's desires is key to promoting harmony in relationships, as it brings happiness to both partners.

99.5 The multiplicity of desires can be a powerful tool for promoting harmony in relationships.

99.6 A deep respect for the other sex should be cultivated, as we rely on each other for survival and fulfil

99.7 lament of desires.

99.8 Modern advancements in contraception and fertility have allowed us greater control over our mating behaviours, but our evolutionary past remains important to understanding where we came from and where we are going.

99.9 Human sexual strategies are living fossils that define our species and inform our destiny.

Women's Hidden Sexual Strategies

100. Human mating strategies are complex and difficult to fully comprehend.

100.1 Women's strategies for achieving their desires are particularly intricate and often hidden.

100.2 Certain strategies are kept secret for evolutionary reasons, as their success may be compromised if revealed.

100.3 Despite this, there is a deep desire to understand women's mating strategies.

100.4 Men may appear more transparent in comparison, but this may be misleading due to co-evolution.

100.5 Women's adaptations to mating are mirrored in the counter-adaptations of men, and vice versa.

100.6 Recent research has focused on four enigmas related to women's mating strategies: the function of the female orgasm, infidelity, links between sexual strategies and the menstrual cycle, and men's ability to detect ovulation in women.

100.7 The language and assumptions used in discussions of love and desire may shape our understanding of these concepts, potentially limiting or distorting them.

100.8 To better understand these concepts, concrete examples and a critical approach to language use and assumptions may be necessary.

101. In a scene from Six Feet Under, Brenda engages in a sexual encounter that turns out to be a fantasy, highlighting the complexities of love, desire, and illusion.

101.1   Female orgasm is a phenomenon that has been studied by scientists for centuries, with varying degrees of success.

101.2   The experience of female orgasm varies considerably across women and is described in a variety of ways, from heightened excitement and muscular tension to slow, deep sensations.

101.3   Despite its complexity, female orgasm has been the subject of much fascination and debate, with some questioning its evolutionary purpose.

101.4   Some argue that female orgasm is a non-adaptive by-product of the male orgasm, while others suggest it may serve a specific function, such as signalling fertility or paternity.

101.5   Ethnographic evidence of female orgasm is limited and often inaccurate, and the variability of female orgasm within and across cultures is not evidence against its adaptation.

101.6   Whether female orgasm is an adaptation or a by-product remains a subject of ongoing scientific inquiry.

102. There are five proposed adaptive functions for female orgasm.

102.1   The hedonic hypothesis suggests that orgasm motivates women to have intercourse throughout their cycle, increasing the likelihood of successful conception. However, empirical variability renders this hypothesis unsupported.

102.2   The Mr. Right hypothesis proposes that female orgasm serves as a mate selection device, allowing women to choose a man who will invest in her and her children. Variability in female orgasm is necessary for this function.

102.3   The paternity confidence hypothesis suggests that female orgasm signals sexual fidelity, leading to increased investment from her mate. However, there are conceptual and empirical problems with this hypothesis.

102.4   The paternity confusion hypothesis proposes that female orgasm evolved to promote promiscuous mating, reducing the odds of infanticide and increasing positive investments from multiple males. However, this hypothesis is untested and has conceptual flaws.

102.5   The sperm retention hypothesis suggests that female orgasm functions to draw sperm into the cervix and uterine cavity, increasing the odds of conception.

102.6   The occurrence of female orgasm varies widely among different cultures.

102.7   Female orgasm may have evolved as a by-product and was adaptively modified to influence when and with whom it occurs.

102.8   Men's sexual strategies may have co-evolved with female orgasm, but there is currently no evidence to support this hypothesis.

103.A study of 349 individuals found that 87% reported having sexual fantasies about someone other than their regular partner within the past two months, with women reporting this experience almost as frequently as men.

103.1   Sexual fantasies motivate individuals to act on their desires when the opportunity arises and the moment is right.

103.2   Women are more likely to have extra-pair sexual fantasies than men, which may encourage them to seek sex in the arms of a lover.

103.3   Women face many potential costs and risks in having affairs, including abandonment by their mate, physical and psychological abuse, damage to their social reputation, impairing their mate value, endangering their children, and contracting sexually transmitted diseases.

103.4   Despite these costs, women still have affairs, and hypotheses have been advanced to explain why.

103.5   One hypothesis is the "good genes" hypothesis, which suggests that women can secure genes from an affair partner that are superior to those of her regular partner.

103.6   Another potential benefit is the leverage to switch to alternative mates, which may permit a "trial run" with another man to secure information about how compatible they are or how much he is willing to invest in her.

103.7   Affairs also might allow a woman to evaluate how desirable she is on the mating market.

103.8   A study found that women choose symmetrical men as affair partners more than asymmetrical men, possibly indicating that women are selecting partners with genes that ultimately increase the survival and reproductive success of their children.

103.9   The language we use to describe love and desire can shape our understanding of these concepts, and our assumptions about them may limit or distort our understanding.

103.10   Recent research supports the mate switching hypothesis.

103.11   Women who have affairs gain various benefits, including sexual gratification and mate switching.

103.12   In mate switching, women seek a partner more desirable than their current partner, find it easier to break up with the current partner, and discover potential partners who are interested in them.

103.13   Women judge mate switching circumstances to be highly likely to trigger an affair.

103.14   Women who have an active history of short-term mating perceive discovering other available partners and partners who are interested in them as huge benefits of affairs.

103.15   Women's affairs provide a boost to their self-esteem by making them feel desirable, intelligent, interesting, beautiful, and sexy.

103.16   Self-esteem benefits give women the psychological self-assurance they need to switch mates.

103.17   Attachment styles play a role in the probability of having an affair.

103.18   Avoidant women are less likely to have an affair, while anxious/ambivalent women are more likely to have affairs.

103.19   Affairs for anxious/ambivalent women serve a mate switching function.

103.20   Women have affairs to obtain investment from one man and superior DNA from another, or to propel themselves out of one relationship in their quest for intimacy in another.

104. Research indicates that women with regular partners experience sexual attraction to other men just before ovulation.

104.1   The qualities of the men women are attracted to during ovulation were explored using digital facial images manipulated to appear more masculine or feminine.

104.2   Women in their least fertile phase of their cycle were most attracted to slightly feminised faces, while women in their most fertile phase were drawn to 30 percent masculinised faces.

104.3   The masculinity of a man's face is a reliable physical marker of immunocompetence, indicating that men with above-average secondary sexual characteristics are extremely healthy and can bear the costs of producing testosterone during development.

104.4   Women's preference for masculinised faces at ovulation reveals a preference for "good genes" that are sometimes better secured from affair partners than from regular mates.

104.5   Women judge less masculine faces as a signal of cooperativeness, honesty, and good parenting qualities and may find these "good guy" qualities most attractive in regular mates.

104.6   A computer program was developed to locate the most attractive face for a short-term mate.

104.7   Women overall, regardless of menstrual phase, preferred faces in the more masculine direction over average faces.

104.8   Women in the high-risk-of-conception phase preferred even more masculine faces than those they preferred during their low-risk phase.

104.9   Women who scored low on a psychological test of "masculinity" showed an especially strong preference shift across their cycle towards masculine-looking males, especially as short-term mating partners.

104.10 Masculine features are primarily a consequence of pubertal hormones and signal good health.

104.11 Women are attracted to healthy, immunocompetent men, especially when fertile and especially for short-term mating, as a means of securing good genes that can be passed down to their children.

105. Bad smell can act as a sexual kill switch, while scent is often seen as central to sexual desire in women.

105.1 Chemical signals play a crucial role in human mating, including the detection of odours and pheromones through olfactory mechanisms.

105.2 Pheromones are chemical messengers secreted by one person's body that can produce physiological and behavioural changes in another person.

105.3 Women have a stronger sense of smell than men, with olfactory acuity peaking at or just prior to ovulation.

105.4 Women judge the body odour of symmetrical men as more pleasant smelling, but only during ovulation.

105.5 Body odour may have other important functions in human mating, but these effects may be muted in modern societies due to regular bathing and deodorant use.

105.6 Women's sexual cycles have subtle rhythms that direct their sexual strategies, which can be influenced by factors such as ovulation.

106. The question arises as to whether men can detect the various aspects of women's mating strategies that are

influenced by ovulation, sexual desire, sexual fantasies, attraction to symmetrical men, and preferences for masculine faces.

106.1 The conventional scientific view is that men cannot detect ovulation and find ovulating women more sexually attractive, although this contradicts simple reproductive logic and the study of nonhuman animals.

106.2 There are, however, compelling adaptive reasons why men should have evolved the ability to detect ovulation.

106.3 Men who could detect when women ovulate could maximise their chances of successful fertilisation and reproduction, while avoiding the opportunity costs of mating effort on non-ovulating women.

106.4 Men's tactics of mate guarding would be most beneficial when directed toward a mate who is ovulating, making lapses in vigilance most costly at that time.

106.5 These adaptive benefits for men would have been operative over the vast expanse of time in which humans evolved, due to the rarity of ovulatory episodes in ancestral women's lives.

106.6 Women's ovulation has become relatively cryptic, but it would defy reproductive logic if men stood evolutionarily still while signs of ovulation were driven underground.

106.7 Recent research has shown that men do detect ovulation through subtle visual and olfactory signals emitted by women.

106.8 Women experience greater sexual desire when ovulating, wear tighter clothes, show more skin, and initiate more sex, while men ramp up their efforts to guard their partners at this time.

106.9 Given the monumental importance of ovulation for reproduction, it would be astonishing if women and men had failed to evolve specific mating strategies to grapple with the adaptive challenges posed by this critical event.

106.10 Mating research is now entering an "ovulation revolution," destined to discover other facets of mating strategies that are tethered to the menstrual cycle.

Mysteries of Human Mating

107. Homosexuality poses a mystery to scientists, as it appears to contradict evolutionary principles. The procreative purpose of the body seems at odds with desires that do not lead to reproduction.

107.1 Rape presents another enigma, with little systematic research to inform our understanding. The debate over whether it is an evolved sexual strategy, a by-product of other adaptations, or a product of modern society continues. The question of anti-rape adaptations in women is also of practical and theoretical significance.

107.2 Other mysteries of mating include gender biases in reading sexual desires, "mate poaching," and the transition from friendship to rivalry. Recent scientific studies have provided insight into these complex issues.

107.3 Our language and assumptions about love and desire may limit or distort our understanding of these concepts. Concrete examples and a critical approach are needed to uncover the ways in which our language use shapes our understanding of the world.

108. Heterosexual orientation is a prevalent psychological adaptation among sexually reproducing species, with the majority of men and women exhibiting a primary orientation towards heterosexuality.

108.1 The existence of a small percentage of primarily or exclusively homosexual individuals poses an evolutionary puzzle, given the lower rates of reproduction among homosexual men.

108.2 The kin altruism theory, which posits that genes for homosexual orientation can evolve and be maintained through increased investment in genetic relatives, encounters conceptual and empirical problems, including a lack of evidence for increased investment in kin among homosexual men.

108.3   The alliance-formation theory proposes that homoerotic behaviour evolved to strengthen same-sex bonds, providing benefits such as access to resources and protection from aggression, but also encounters several problems, including a lack of evidence for the universality of same-sex sexual behaviour and exclusive homosexual orientation, and the existence of same-sex non-sexual alliances.

108.4   The language and assumptions used in discussing love and desire may limit or distort our understanding of these concepts, and scientific theories about their origins and persistence should be critically examined in light of empirical data.

108.5   Homosexuality may be a by-product of genes designed for producing "feminine" traits in men, making them more attractive to women as better parents and providers.

108.6   Possessing a moderate number of "good guy" genes gives men an optimal mix of masculinity and femininity that is attractive to women.

108.7   Homosexuality occurs in a small percentage of men who draw an unusually large number of "feminine" traits from their genetic lottery.

108.8   The nice-guy theory of homosexuality faces conceptual and empirical difficulties, as there are no modifier genes that allow niceness to coexist with heterosexuality.

108.9 Empirical evidence suggests that women do not prefer men with "feminine" traits over men with more "masculine" traits.

108.10 Existing theories of homosexuality fail to explain lesbianism and contain fundamental conceptual and empirical problems.

108.11 The possibility of a "gay gene" has not been confirmed, and other theories suggest that homosexuality may be a by-product of novel modern environments.

108.12 Homosexuality is not a singular phenomenon, with lesbianism and male homosexuality having different natures and developmental trajectories.

108.13 Women's sexual orientation is more flexible over the life span, with a continuum from highly heterosexual to same-sex partners.

108.14 Future theories should respect the different natures of lesbianism and male homosexuality and attend to large individual differences within those currently classified as "lesbian" and "gay."

108.15 Despite recent attention to understanding and explaining homosexuality, their origins remain scientific mysteries with profound individual differences among those with same-sex sexual orientation.

109. A circulated memo via email suggests different ways to attract a mate for men and women.

109.1 The joke may not accurately reflect women's desire for sexual variety, but it reveals a significant difference between men and women's evolved sexual strategies.

109.2   Research shows that men generally have a stronger desire for a variety of sexual partners than women.

109.3   Men are also more likely to engage in casual sex than women.

109.4   Women engage in short-term mating, but their motives for doing so differ from men.

109.5   Men who have had many sexual partners are emotionally stable and score higher on self-esteem.

109.6   Men's desire for sexual variety decreases with age, while women's remains constant.

109.7   Women who are prostitutes are underrepresented in sex surveys, which explains the discrepancy between men and women's reported number of sexual partners.

109.8   Both men and women have a range of sexual strategies, from casual sex to lifelong monogamy.

109.9   It is established that men worldwide have a greater desire for sexual variety than women, but attempts to reduce human mating to a single strategy are not reflective of reality.

110. The movie "When Harry Met Sally" explores the idea that men and women cannot be friends without the possibility of sex getting in the way.

110.1   However, a female colleague's experience shows that men and women can form close friendships without any sexual desire, but sometimes misunderstandings can lead to the end of the friendship.

110.2   Evolutionary psychologist April Bleske conducted a study on opposite-sex friendships and found that men are more likely to desire sex with their female friends than women are with their male friends.

110.3   Men often wrongly perceive their female friends as sexually attracted to them, leading to misperceptions and potentially the end of the friendship.

110.4   While some opposite-sex friendships may turn into sexual relationships, most remain platonic, with women not reciprocating their male friends' sexual desires.

110.5   In conclusion, while men and women can form close friendships, they must be aware of potential misperceptions and misunderstandings that may arise from sexual desire.

111.Same-sex friends occupy a unique position in our social lives, offering benefits such as protection, valuable information, and advice.

111.1   Friends have special knowledge of our strengths and vulnerabilities, and can hurt us in ways that enemies cannot.

111.2   Similarity and propinquity are fundamental laws of mating, drawing friends and mates together.

111.3   Friends are well positioned to become sexual Trojan Horses, using the guise of friendship to poach mates.

111.4   Mate poaching is a severe problem in same-sex friendships, with the most frequent instances involving deception about mating-related issues.

111.5   Women are particularly aware of same-sex sexual deception, and may intentionally lowball their sexual experience to avoid seeming like a threat to committed relationships.

111.6　True friends enrich life, but they are also in a position to betray and deceive, risking the loss of both friendship and romantic partnership.

112. Desirable mates are scarce, especially those who are attractive, interesting, and socially skilled.

112.1　Those who do attract desirable partners tend to hold onto them tightly, and transitions between relationships for the beautiful are brief.

112.2　Mate shortages become more severe each passing year for those left on the sidelines of the mating pool.

112.3　In traditional polygynous societies, single men suffer the most, as most desirable women marry shortly after puberty.

112.4　Mate poaching is a common strategy used to acquire a desirable mate, despite being viewed as loathsome by many.

112.5　People poach for many of the same reasons they seek a mate, but perceive additional benefits unique to the context of mate poaching, such as gaining revenge against a rival.

112.6　Mate poachers use similar tactics to attract a mate as they would in other contexts, but also employ strategies such as temporal invasion and driving a wedge.

112.7　Mate poaching carries risks, such as violence, damage to social reputation, and the potential need for increased mate guarding even if successful.

112.8　Our language and assumptions about love and desire may limit or distort our understanding of these concepts, as evidenced by the prevalence of mate poaching as a mating strategy.

113. Human mating is fraught with sexual treachery and both sexes indulge in sexual fantasies about other partners.

113.1 Women tend to fantasise more about strangers when ovulating and seek affairs with more desirable men than their regular partners.

113.2 Genetic cuckoldry is a threat to men, while infidelities by men jeopardise women's investment and commitment.

113.3 Sexual and emotional infidelity can both result in significant loss of reproductively valuable resources.

113.4 Men tend to be more distressed by sexual infidelity, while women tend to be more distressed by emotional infidelity.

113.5 These sex differences have been found across diverse cultures and have been supported by empirical tests.

113.6 The defence against infidelity includes not just jealousy, but other design features such as mate guarding.

113.7 Men tend to mate guard intensely when married to young and physically attractive women, while women tend to mate guard more intensely when married to men with abundant resources and status.

113.8 The defence of jealousy is an evolved solution to the problem of maintaining relationships despite the ever-present threat of sexual betrayal and emotional defection.

113.9 Another dark threat to women and their partners is the abhorrent possibility of rape.

114. Across cultures, women are at risk of being raped, regardless of their location.

114.1   Rape can also occur in non-human primates, such as orangutans.

114.2   In the year 2000, Thornhill and Palmer published a book that ignited controversy as it proposed the theory that rape is an evolutionary adaptation, outlining six specialised adaptations for men that may have evolved.

114.3   Direct evidence against the mate deprivation hypothesis of rape is highlighted through a study conducted on 1.56 heterosexual men.

114.4   It has been found that women of reproductive age are most likely to be victims of rape.

114.5   Research into the causes of rape is limited and ideologically charged, making it difficult to gain a comprehensive understanding of the phenomenon.

114.6   The classification of different types of rape is necessary for a better understanding of its causes, and different types of rape may have distinct causes.

115.Rape is a pervasive fear for women, deeply embedded in their understanding of the natural environment.

115.1   The debate on rape has largely focused on the motivations of the rapist, with little attention paid to the psychological impact on victims.

115.2   All sides agree that rape is a heinous act that imposes significant costs on victims.

115.3   From an evolutionary perspective, rape undermines female sexual strategy by bypassing their choice in sexual partners and risking pregnancy with a genetically inferior mate.

115.4 Victims of rape suffer psychologically, experiencing a range of negative emotions and isolation.

115.5 Socially, rape victims may be blamed for the crime, suffer damage to their reputation, and become socially shunned.

115.6 Despite these costs, rape has occurred throughout human history, and we can only make educated guesses about whether anti-rape defences have evolved in women.

115.7 The cross-cultural evidence shows that rape is reported in many traditional societies.

115.8 Given the catastrophic costs of rape, it would be illogical for evolutionary selection not to have fashioned defences in women to prevent its occurrence.

116. Male violence against women is prevalent across cultures, and societies with low rates of violence are exceptions.

116.1 Evolutionary scientists have proposed potential evolved defences against rape, including specialised fears and risk-avoidance strategies.

116.2 Ovulating women show a decrease in risk-taking activities, indicating the possibility of specialised risk-avoidance as an anti-rape adaptation.

116.3 Women routinely engage in risk-avoidance manoeuvres to prevent harm, such as isolation and street-savvy tactics.

116.4 Women's fears of rape do not always match the reality of rape, but may motivate precautionary behaviours that prevent rape.

116.5 Women may form heterosexual pair bonds with men as a defence against sexual aggression from other men, a hypothesis known as the bodyguard hypothesis.

116.6   Specialised psychological pain may motivate women to avoid similar recurrences of rape in the future.

116.7   Research on women's anti-rape strategies and their effectiveness is urgently needed to determine if they are evolved adaptations or products of general mechanisms.

117. Humans inhabit a socially uncertain world, where inferences about others' emotional states and intentions must be made.

117.1   Such inferences are complicated by concealed states, including passions for others, which give rise to a multitude of cues.

117.2   In reading others' minds, two types of error can occur: inferring a non-existent psychological state, or failing to infer a present one.

117.3   Error Management Theory, proposed by evolutionary psychologist Martie Haselton, highlights the asymmetries in the cost-benefit consequences of such errors.

117.4   As a result, predictably biased cognitive mechanisms for reading others' minds are produced.

117.5   Haselton and others have identified two biases: the sexual over-perception bias in men, and the commitment scepticism bias in women.

117.6   These biases have arisen from selection pressures over evolutionary time, and reflect functional adaptations rather than flaws in psychological mechanisms.

117.7 Error Management Theory provides a novel perspective on mating problems, enabling men and women to better read each other's mating minds.

118. The existence of adaptations to sperm competition in humans is not fully understood.

118.1 Some research has found evidence of psychological adaptations related to sperm competition, such as increased sexual desire when separated from one's mate.

118.2 Further research may uncover both physiological and psychological adaptations related to sperm competition.

118.3 Incest avoidance is a prime example of aversions playing a role in mating.

118.4 The near-universal aversion to genetic relatives may have evolved due to the costs of inbreeding and the benefits of outbreeding.

118.5 Numerous studies have confirmed the sexual aversion and emotional disgust experienced towards genetic relatives.

118.6 Future research may investigate the mechanisms of incest avoidance and the consequences of violating the incest taboo.

118.7 Mate value influences mate selection preferences, with more desirable individuals imposing higher standards.

118.8 Budget allocation methods have shown that individuals with higher mate value pursue more "luxuries" in mate selection.

118.9 Individual differences in mate value have obvious implications for sexual strategies and potential mates available.

118.10 Further research may explore the subtler implications of mate value, such as its relationship to reproductive cycles and power dynamics within relationships.

119. The human quest for successful mating is a product of evolution by selection, resulting in complex and elaborate mechanisms.

119.1 Mating plays a central role in various human endeavours, including forming friendships, derogating competitors, pursuing prestige, and motivating murder.

119.2 Verbal signals used in attraction, humour, courtship, and sexual gossip are a product of the evolution of language.

119.3 The evolution of large game hunting and the physical and psychological adaptations it required enabled greater provisioning in courtship.

119.4 Various aspects of human anatomy, physiology, psychology, and cultural traditions have been refined by the successes and failures of our hominid ancestors in mating.

119.5 Mating influences all social relationships, with men misreading women's smiles for sexual exploitation and women remaining sceptical of men's commitment signals to avoid sexual victimisation.

119.6 Fathers and daughters manipulate each other to influence mate choice, and both sexes deploy deceptive signals in mating.

119.7 Same-sex allies can turn into Trojan horses, and late poachers hide behind smiling faces.

119.8   Mating permeates much of what we do as individuals, and as a species, it defines who we are.

Published by Lulu Press, Inc
627 Davis Drive Suite 300
Morrisville, NC 27560
United States

+1 844 212 0689
www.lulu.com

ISBN: 978-1-326-48219-0